SOCIAL JUSTICE AND CULTURALLY RELEVANT PREVENTION

Other Books in the Prevention Practice Kit

Program Development and Evaluation in Prevention (9781452258010)

Prevention and Consultation (9781452257990)

Prevention in Psychology (9781452257952)

Prevention Groups (9781452257983)

Public Policy and Mental Health (9781452258027)

Evidence-Based Prevention (9781452258003)

Best Practices in Prevention (9781452257976)

To the counseling psychologists and members of the APA Division 17 prevention section who are dedicated to prevention and social justice.

SOCIAL JUSTICE AND CULTURALLY RELEVANT PREVENTION

ELIZABETH M. VERA
Loyola University Chicago

MAUREEN E. KENNY
Boston College

Los Angeles | London | New Delhi
Singapore | Washington DC

Los Angeles | London | New Delhi
Singapore | Washington DC

FOR INFORMATION:

SAGE Publications, Inc.
2455 Teller Road
Thousand Oaks, California 91320
E-mail: order@sagepub.com

SAGE Publications Ltd.
1 Oliver's Yard
55 City Road
London EC1Y 1SP
United Kingdom

SAGE Publications India Pvt. Ltd.
B 1/I 1 Mohan Cooperative Industrial Area
Mathura Road, New Delhi 110 044
India

SAGE Publications Asia-Pacific Pte. Ltd.
3 Church Street
#10-04 Samsung Hub
Singapore 049483

Acquisitions Editor: Kassie Graves
Editorial Assistant: Elizabeth Luizzi
Production Editor: Brittany Bauhaus
Copy Editor: QuADS Prepress (P) Ltd.
Typesetter: C&M Digitals (P) Ltd.
Proofreader: Jeff Bryant
Indexer: Diggs Publication Services, Inc.
Cover Designer: Glenn Vogel
Marketing Manager: Lisa Sheldon Brown
Permissions Editor: Adele Hutchinson

Copyright © 2013 by SAGE Publications, Inc.

Printed in the United States of America

Library of Congress Cataloging-in-Publication Data

Social justice and culturally relevant prevention / editors, Elizabeth M. Vera and Maureen E. Kenny.

p. cm. — (Prevention practice kit)
Includes bibliographical references and index.

ISBN 978-1-4522-5796-9 (pbk.)

1. Social justice. 2. Preventive health services.
I. Vera, Elizabeth, 1967- II. Kenny, Maureen.

HM671.S6533 2013
303.3'72—dc23   2012040371

This book is printed on acid-free paper.

12 13 14 15 16 10 9 8 7 6 5 4 3 2 1

Brief Contents _____

Detailed Contents _____

Acknowledgments_____

A sincere thank you to our colleagues who collaborate in our endeavors to offer culturally relevant, social justice–driven prevention projects. Specifically, many thanks to the faculty and students at Loyola University Chicago, who have for many years supported prevention efforts to communities in need. Also, thanks to David Blustein and other Boston College colleagues and graduate students and public school teachers and students who engaged in the second case study presented in this chapter. Thanks also to Mary Beth Medvide for assistance in the literature review.

Introduction _____

Social justice and cultural relevance have become increasingly popular topics in the prevention literature. Scholarship on these topics is also becoming more commonplace throughout the gamut of mental health professions, suggesting that an agenda that includes social justice and cultural relevance may be a significant trend in the 21st century. This trend is long overdue for reasons that will be explored throughout this volume. However, understanding the importance of social justice and cultural relevance to the field of prevention begins with a delineation of the ways in which these concepts have been defined in the existing mental health literature.

A variety of definitions of social justice exist, most of which emphasize ideals of equity and liberty (Stevens & Wood, 1992), but a frequently cited definition is provided by Bell (2007): The goal of social justice entails

> full and equal participation of all groups in a society that is mutually shaped to meet their needs. Social justice includes a vision of society in which the distribution of resources is equitable and all members are physically and psychologically safe and secure. (p. 3)

This definition emphasizes equitable outcomes as well as collaborative processes that lead to justice. Cultural relevance refers to the extent to which interventions are consistent with the values, beliefs, and desired outcomes of a particular community (Kumpfer, Alvarado, Smith, & Bellamy, 2002; Nation et al., 2003). Many prevention scholars have argued that cultural relevance is a hallmark of effective prevention programs (Hage et al., 2007; Vera, 2000). We would argue that engaging in democratic, collaborative processes of identifying and responding to community needs is one prerequisite of culturally relevant prevention efforts aimed at promoting social justice.

Culturally relevant, social justice–oriented prevention must embrace processes that support collaboration with our participants. Such processes are "democratic and participatory, inclusive and affirming of human agency and human capacity for working collaboratively to create change" (Bell, 2007, p. 4). Such prevention, then, is not only concerned with combating inequities such as racial disparities in the juvenile justice system (i.e., an outcome), but it seeks to create access to and equity in social and political power, which is often at the heart of liberating oppressed groups. A lack of such power, also known as marginalization, is the main process that maintains socially unjust societies around the world. Young (1990) argued that in the United States, a large proportion of the population is expelled from full participation in social and political life, including the poor, people of color, the elderly, the disabled, women, gay men, lesbians, bisexual people, and people who are involuntarily out of work. Thus, issues of social justice are important for the statistical majority of the population in this country. Such a conceptualization of justice is by definition related to issues of multiculturalism and diversity in that multiculturalism cannot flourish without notions of justice and equality (Albee, 2000; Helms & Cook, 1999; Martin-Baró, 1994; Ramirez, 1999; Vera & Speight, 2003).

We will argue throughout this volume that culturally relevant prevention is a critical component to a social justice agenda for mental health professionals. Historically, prevention has been a far less popular activity for mental health professionals than has been remedial approaches such as psychotherapy. Although remedial counseling efforts are aimed at reducing human suffering and empowering clients, attributes shared with prevention efforts, they fall short in truly adhering to a social justice agenda. The limitations of remedial counseling relate to the impact, access, and often incongruence of traditional therapies with the social and cultural values of diverse groups (Vera, Buhin, & Isacco, 2009). Because treatment is not offered until after a problem occurs, remedial counseling is limited in the extent to which human suffering is ever prevented. Remedial treatment does nothing to reduce the incidence of new mental health problems but seeks to eliminate the distress and dysfunction of persons who are already diagnosed with mental health difficulties (Albee, 2000). In addition, as noted by many authors (e.g., Albee, 2000; Vera & Speight, 2003), remedial approaches tend to support the status quo or exacerbate conditions associated with social injustice because they typically fail to address the underlying social conditions or injustices that contribute to psychological disorders in favor of addressing individual and/or family dynamics that contribute to such problems. Furthermore, even if remedial therapy did focus on addressing larger social conditions such as poverty, racism, and heterosexism that are associated with many psychological and physical disorders, those who are marginalized (i.e., economically and socially disadvantaged) are least likely to have access to quality health and mental health care (Agency for Healthcare Research and Quality, 2008). African Americans in the United States, for example, are overrepresented in low-income groups, are less likely to have health insurance, are more likely to live in unsafe neighborhoods, and exhibit more unhealthy behaviors, resulting in lower life expectancies than those of Whites (Weisfeld & Perlman, 2005). A social justice perspective would argue that the primary factors contributing to health disparities are rooted in discrimination, poverty, and other forms of oppression (Speight & Vera, 2008). These root factors, in turn, affect the community environment (e.g., higher rates of unemployment), behavioral factors (e.g., diet, exercise, tobacco use), and ultimately result in a higher need for medical services (Giles & Liburd, 2007). This injustice is further exacerbated by the fact that there are not enough available quality and affordable health services to meet the needs of those who may need the greatest amount of help. For example, it is estimated that anywhere from 9% to 20% of children experience social and emotional problems that negatively affect their functioning and development (Brauner & Stephen, 2006; Costello et al., 1996). However, research suggests that current mental health services meet the needs of only 31% of nonminority children and 13% of minority group children (Ringel & Sturm, 2001).

While efforts have been made to make remedial treatment more culturally relevant and to increase the cultural competence of mental health professionals (Constantine, Hage, Kindaichi, & Bryant, 2007; Crethar, Rivera, & Nash, 2008), communities who might truly benefit from such interventions remain disproportionately underserved. A factor which compounds this social injustice is that psychotherapy remains incongruous with the values of many racial and ethnic groups who view mental health treatment as stigmatizing or who may lack trust in mental health professionals (Sue & Sue, 1999). Help seeking may traditionally be sought from indigenous healers, family members, and other community members who share a common language and cultural values (Atkinson, Thompson, & Grant, 1993; Constantine et al., 2007). Linguistic barriers may also limit participation in traditional psychotherapy when the availability of bilingual mental health professionals is limited (Constantine et al., 2007). As noted by Vera, Daly, Gonzales, Morgan, and Thakral (2006), the numerous barriers that impede access to quality services among underserved groups make a strong case for the expansion of services to be offered to such communities, including prevention.

Albee (2000), a community psychologist and former president of the American Psychological Association, was one of the field's earliest advocates for social justice. Albee embraced prevention as a means for reducing the social conditions that contribute to social injustice. Integral to Albee's understanding of prevention as a mechanism for social justice is an emphasis on the role of oppression and social inequality as causal factors in physical and mental illness (Trickett, 2007). In addition to reducing oppression, social change might also be directed toward enhancing positive environmental conditions, such as access to quality education, safe recreation centers, and other basic necessities that support healthy lifestyles. In sum, we believe that for prevention to be grounded in social justice, it should seek to eliminate forces of oppression through systemic change and also support the development of those individual and community assets that foster self-determination and the attainment of community goals (Kenny & Romano, 2009). Incorporating community assets and goals is thus emblematic of culturally relevant prevention.

In spite of what could be argued is considerable recent enthusiasm for multicultural and social justice issues in the mental health fields, there are only now emerging detailed writings on the practicality of infusing social justice and cultural relevance into prevention efforts (Reese & Vera, 2007). Therefore, the purpose of this volume is threefold. First, we aim to review the relevant literature, both theoretical and empirical, on social justice and cultural relevance within the field of prevention. Second, we will describe concrete examples of programs that attempt to address issues of social injustice and cultural relevance. Third, we aspire to provide opportunities for conversation about some of the more challenging aspects of infusing social justice and cultural relevance into one's prevention efforts. We have provided a series of learning exercises to promote these conversations. Our overall goal is to provide the reader with practical information and discussion of real-world challenges and opportunities, all intended to help the reader to discover and dialogue about the complexities inherent in engaging in culturally relevant, social justice–oriented prevention practice and science.

1

Theoretical Conceptualizations of Cultural Relevance and Social Justice

The importance of culture has taken center stage in the mental health professions over the past 20 years. Prior to that time, questions of how culture shaped the psychological experiences of individuals were asked infrequently, and the cultural competence of mental health service providers was rarely discussed. In 1990, Pedersen characterized multiculturalism as the "fourth force" in counseling, referring to its historical importance as a major sea-changing movement. A year later, Speight, Myers, Cox, and Highlen (1991) argued that when one defines culture in an inclusive way (i.e., to include considerations of gender, race, ethnicity, socioeconomic status, sexual orientation, religion, ability status, etc.), then all counseling constitutes multicultural counseling, asserting the relevance of cultural competence to all mental health professionals.

Several subsequent developments in the mental health fields suggest that issues of cultural competence are now part of a national platform for psychologists and mental health professionals. The U.S. Department of Health and Human Services (U.S. DHHS, 2000) identified the elimination of health disparities as the central objective of its Healthy People 2010 campaign. In 2003, the American Psychological Association adopted the Guidelines on Multicultural Education, Training, Research, Practice, and Organizational change for Psychologists. The National Institutes of Health created the National Center on Minority Health and Health Disparities in 2003, whose focus is on improving the health of ethnic minority communities and eliminating health disparities. Likewise, the U.S. Departments of Education and Justice identified initiatives targeting achievement gaps and the overrepresentation of ethnic minority youth in correctional facilities, respectively (Reese & Vera, 2007). Thus, cultural competencies in the delivery of mental health services have indeed moved from the margin to a more central role in our profession.

However, for as much enthusiasm that has been observed for cultural issues in the literature, one might wonder whether service delivery has become more effective in improving the lives of historically marginalized populations within the United States. Unfortunately, there are still many cultural health disparities that suggest that our efforts to meet the needs of diverse cultural groups are far from done. As discussed by Reese and Vera (2007), homicide has been the leading cause of death for African Americans between the ages of 15 and 34 for the past decade and the second leading cause of death for Latinos (Centers for Disease Control and Prevention [CDC], 2005). In our nation's schools, Latinos continue to have the lowest rates of high school completion and the highest rates of dropout (Harvard Civil Rights Project, 2004). Ethnic minority youth, especially African American and Latino, have been disproportionately arrested and convicted of crimes and constitute 70% of all juvenile inmates, despite the fact that they make up only 30% of such youth (CDC, 2005). These data suggest that there is still an alarming need for the mental health field to support large-scale initiatives aimed at addressing the risk factors facing historically underserved populations.

As noted by Conyne and Horne (Book 1 in this volume), the identification of risk and protective factors at varied levels of the ecological context (Bronfenbrenner, 1979) provides a useful framework for understanding the multiple determinants of behavior. As a guide for prevention, many interventions are designed to reduce risks at the individual, family, school, community, and societal levels. An exclusive focus on risk, however, may neglect the variety of social and cultural strengths that characterize ethnic minority youth, their families, and their communities. Prevention efforts that seek to promote social justice are complex. While attention should be directed toward reducing risks, such as community-level violence, unemployment, and racial discrimination that are prevalent beyond the individual, prevention should also seek to enhance culturally relevant strengths and assets that can serve to protect the individual from societal risks and promote capacity for engaging fully in society (Kenny & Romano, 2009).

Ethnic and racial health disparities as described above have contributed to more recent conversations in our field about social injustices and the extent to which mental health professionals are answering a call to a social justice agenda. Vera and Speight (2003) argued that the multicultural competence movement has, in fact, not focused enough on social justice. They argued that a paradigm shift was in order, one that would prioritize activities such as prevention, outreach, and advocacy. There have been many other scholars who have echoed these sentiments. In the past 8 years, for example, scholars have published several major contributions to the literature on the application of a social justice agenda to the conceptualization of multicultural competence (Speight & Vera, 2004; Vera & Speight, 2003), teaching and training (Goodman et al., 2004), and vocational psychology (Blustein, McWhirter, & Perry, 2005). The most definitive culminations of this work appear in the *Handbook for Social Justice in Counseling Psychology* (Toporek, Gerstein, Fouad, Roysircar, & Israel, 2006), which contains 35 chapters on applications of social justice research and practice, and *Realizing Social Justice: The Challenge for Preventive Interventions* (Kenny, Horne, Orpinas, & Reese, 2009a), which contains 13 chapters that specifically focus on the importance of prevention for a social justice agenda within the mental health fields.

Prior to these more recent contributions, social justice–oriented approaches to mental health service delivery were being promoted by a handful of scholars. In addition to the pioneering work of Albee, two models of mental health practice that included social justice–driven interventions (e.g., advocacy, prevention) were proposed by Atkinson et al. (1993) and Lewis, Lewis, D'Andrea, and Daniels (1999). Both these models identified a wide range of activities that either directly or indirectly serve to address the mental health needs of clients. Prevention activities can fall into both direct and indirect intervention categories, whereas advocacy would be an example of indirect service.

Direct interventions in these models included activities where clinicians work directly with clients using interventions such as psychoeducation or skill building, both of which could be part of a prevention program. An example of prevention that would fall under the category of an indirect intervention would be a parenting group for children who are at risk for violent behavior. The intervention in this case will affect the clients (i.e., the children) indirectly by improving the parenting they receive. Advocacy is another example of an indirect intervention. Trusty and Brown (2005) and Field and Baker (2004) define advocacy as identifying unmet needs and taking actions to change the circumstances that contribute to a problem or inequity. Hence, advocates plead the cause of another or defend causes. Advocacy involves working to change institutionalized policies and practices that impede the well-being of others as to promote equity of opportunities for education, health, and other basic human rights. Kiselica and Robinson (2001) supported this idea with their definition of advocacy counseling as an approach to counseling in which the counselor goes beyond the traditional verbal interventions to identify ways in which constituents' voices are not heard or are devalued.

A clinician who advocates for legislation that increases access to mental health services for first offenders in the criminal justice system would be attempting to prevent youths from reentering the system. In this example, advocacy is a form of prevention aimed at changing policies that perpetrate injustices within a system. If the policies are amended and juvenile first-time offenders were referred to mental health services, the likelihood of an individual reoffending would be minimized. This type of action is very much in line with a social justice orientation to prevention.

The aforementioned counseling models defined ways in which mental health professionals could expand their roles to include activities that affected larger systems, which is consistent with a social justice approach. Prior to this, arguments for the expansion of these roles were offered by Gottlieb (1975), who proposed the addition of the "advocate professional" to the scientist–practitioner training model. As Fouad, Gerstein, and Toporek (2006) noted, early pioneers in the counseling field focused their social advocacy efforts on vocational issues for the poor, individuals with disabilities, women, veterans, and minorities. However, contemporary commitments to issues of social justice have been described as "waxing and waning over time" (p. 12).

So while prevention has been lauded for its role in a social justice–oriented agenda for mental health professionals, Kenny, Horne, Orpinas, and Reese (2009b) argued that prevention has yet to fulfill its social justice promise. Most prevention has targeted the amelioration of individual and/or familial factors that predict the emergence of mental health problems. Utilizing prevention efforts to affect disparities and address social conditions that cause and/or exacerbate mental health outcomes is relatively less typical. Part of the challenge of addressing social justice issues in a sustained way may be that it is difficult (a) to identify the underlying reasons that particular groups of individuals are at risk for specific mental health problems and (b) to design interventions that can affect deleterious social conditions that present risk to particular groups (Reese & Vera, 2007).

With regard to identifying the reasons for mental health disparities, there are likely important within-group differences that confound how between-group differences should be interpreted (Reese & Vera, 2007). As one illustration, ethnic group disparities in a given diagnostic category may also be confounded by disparities due to socioeconomic status, immigration status, or other important aspects of culture. If such disparities, then, are either caused or exacerbated by larger societal influences such as poverty, discrimination, or structurally embedded racism, the mental health fields must make efforts to eliminate these conditions and/or minimize their impact on well-being. For example, to the degree that racism and discrimination negatively affect mental health, more large-scale efforts to teach children an appreciation for cultural differences might in time reduce discriminatory and racist actions and promote well-being. Unfortunately, our field has been relatively less active in presenting specific recommendations on which interventions might best dismantle these oppressive forces.

Reese and Vera (2007) argued that to reduce and ultimately eliminate cultural group disparities, culturally relevant preventative interventions that are social justice oriented are a necessity. Many prevention scholars have argued that cultural relevance is a best practice or hallmark of effective prevention programs (Hage et al., 2007). For example, Nation et al. (2003) argued that prevention program relevance is a function of the extent to which a community's norms, cultural beliefs, and practices have been integrated into program content, its delivery, and evaluation. The infusion of cultural characteristics of the participants is an example of deep structural modification, as opposed to surface modifications (Resnicow, Solar, Braithwaite, Ahluwalia, & Butler, 2000). Deep-structure modifications might be accomplished in sexual risk-taking prevention programs by taking into account the different gender-specific motivations that boys and girls have for engaging in sexual activity. The content of the program would specifically address these different motivations (e.g., girls' motivation to not disappoint a romantic partner vs. boys' motivation to prove their masculinity). Surface modifications to existing prevention programs, on the other hand, might include translating more generic types of intervention materials into the primary language of the participants or hiring program staff who have similar sex and ethnic backgrounds to that of the participants. Such modifications may be one aspect of cultural relevance. However, when program content does not reflect the reality of the participants' experience, interventions delivered by racially or linguistically similar staff will not make the program relevant and, more important, effective (Reese & Vera, 2007). Furthermore, when the oppressive forces that may exacerbate particular problems in specific communities are not addressed in prevention programs, then the extent to which social justice is being addressed is questionable at best.

The understanding of the world view of community participants is an essential component of integrating culture into prevention programs (Reese & Vera, 2007). World view is the manner in which an individual, group, or institution understands and relates to the world and its elements. It is informed by constructs such as epistemology (basis of knowledge), axiology (values), and ontology (nature of reality), among other considerations (Myers, 1988). World views that inform the theory and practice of educational and health interventions that are different from those of the communities targeted by the interventions will face challenges to cultural relevance, community participation, and ultimately program effectiveness (Reese, Vera, & Caldwell, 2005). By contrast, Kumpfer et al. (2002) argued that true cultural relevance in prevention programs improves recruitment, retention, and outcome effectiveness.

Obviously, having specific cultural knowledge can minimize the occurrence of cultural bias that prevention professionals may inadvertently interject into the development and implementation strategies they employ in their interventions. For example, Hage (2000) suggested that intimate partner violence prevention practitioners take into account the role of environmental stressors, such as sexism, racism, and poverty, as they affect women's perceptions of their ability to control their environments. Thus, some women may experience increased partner violence in their intimate relationships not only due to feeling disempowered in their romantic relationships but also as a function of disempowerment they experience in the community and the larger society. Conversely, in considering the experiences of men as victims of intimate partner violence as perpetrated by women or the experiences of men and women in same-sex relationships, some of these same assertions may or may not hold true. Thus, obtaining appropriate cultural familiarity must occur in dialogue with the target communities of prevention efforts to increase the likelihood of interventions being effective (Kenny & Romano, 2009; Reese & Vera, 2007).

For prevention to be culturally relevant, investigators must have knowledge of the community to (a) develop positive working relationships with community members and (b) develop and implement programs that are valued by the community (Reese & Vera, 2007). Taking the time to gain familiarity with a particular community is a key prerequisite of successful prevention work because many professionals are "outsiders" to the community members with whom they work (Reiss & Price, 1996). As a result, it may be important to spend time in the community and make contributions valued by the community before, during, and after interventions begin (Kenny & Gallagher, 2000; Lerner, 1995). Examples of such contributions may include volunteering at community events or school functions. Such contributions give researchers an "inside view" of cultural and community norms and also demonstrate a serious level of commitment to the community itself. These preliminary efforts may translate into important social capital and a service delivery plan that is responsive to the needs of, and valued by, the community (Kenny & Gallagher, 2000).

Social justice–oriented, culturally relevant prevention, therefore, can best be conceptualized as informed by the cultural realities of the participants, based on an inclusive process of community collaboration, imbued with content that has face validity, and aimed at "facilitating the empowerment of clients and addressing systemic barriers that limit equal access to opportunities and resources" (Kenny & Romano, 2009, p. 18). In addition, this type of prevention must be strengths based and emphasize building the capacity of individuals and communities to determine their own futures. Cultural bias among professionals can contribute to a view of attitudes and behaviors that differ from one's own as deficits, without recognition of their role as culturally relevant assets. In the next section of this volume, we will provide a summary of the empirical research that has been conducted on prevention programs that aim to incorporate elements of cultural relevancy and/or social justice.

2 Research on Culturally Relevant, Social Justice–Oriented Prevention Efforts Determining Cultural Relevancy

The value of culturally relevant, social justice–oriented prevention efforts has been discussed theoretically or conceptually at length by a host of scholars, as has been demonstrated in the previous section of this volume. Hence, one would expect to find a large body of empirical studies that have been done to identify best practices in implementing such programs as well as efforts to evaluate the effectiveness of programs designed to be culturally relevant and oriented toward social justice. Interestingly, however, when searching for research on "cultural relevance" or research that promotes "social justice," the studies that fall into these categories are often examples of attempts to transport previously designed, empirically supported prevention programs to underserved communities. Such studies are really examining whether traditional prevention approaches can be "transported" into marginalized communities, where there may be great need, in an attempt to address social injustices.

This trend in the research is an extension of the larger movement within the mental health fields toward using manualized, empirically supported treatment strategies (Hoagwood, 2001). The movement emphasizes the identification of "best practices" in treating specific types of disorders. In the prevention field, the movement encourages the identification of programs that are efficacious in controlled settings and then the application of those programs to new populations. Often, these populations are historically marginalized communities in which the incidence of particular problems may be overrepresented statistically. We will review several examples of this type of work and then discuss its merits and limitations. In addition, it is important to examine the standard methodologies used in prevention research to determine how we may best attempt to measure the successes of culturally relevant, social justice–oriented prevention programs.

Another trend in the prevention literature is the transportation of empirically supported prevention programs into culturally diverse communities to examine their effectiveness. Typically in this body of research, the investigators have identified programs found to be efficacious in randomized, controlled studies, and then attempted to see if the program would be effective when used in a new setting, with a population who may differ significantly from the population on which the original program was designed. For example, Barrera and colleagues (2002) conducted an evaluation of a school-based intervention aimed at reducing conduct problems in at-risk Hispanic children (as compared with White children). The intervention itself was an integration of several existing evidence-based treatments for reducing disruptive behaviors (e.g., Incredible Years parenting program, Webster-Stratton, 1992a; Dina Dinosaur Social Skills Program, Webster-Stratton, 1992b). Children in the experimental group demonstrated fewer negative social behaviors when compared with children in the control group, and parents reported fewer coercive and antisocial behaviors in the intervention group as compared with the control group, suggesting that this program may be culturally relevant for Latino populations.

A second example is Multisystemic Therapy (MST), another evidence-based, intensive intervention for families that focuses on improving communication, school performance, parenting skills, and peer relations (Chorpita, 2002; Hoagwood, 2001). MST is designed to address the role of multiple, interconnected systems in which the child is embedded (Henggeler & Lee, 2003). The specific interventions are individualized and based on the needs of the family. Henggeler (1995) designed the program to integrate different family therapy and cognitive behavioral therapy techniques and interventions. Several recent clinical trials support the efficacy of MST with African American juvenile offenders (Huey & Polo, 2008). Thus, it is reasonable to conclude that MST is culturally relevant for African American families with children who evidence conduct disorders. However, given that in many instances, there is a co-occurrence of poverty within the racial groups included in the evaluation, it is difficult to ascertain whether the program would be effective with members of the same racial group who do not share the same socioeconomic status as the study participants. This illustrates some of the complexities of validating interventions as being culturally relevant.

When research determines that programs evidence effectiveness with culturally diverse populations, it is logical to argue that some types of prevention approaches may be "universally" applicable, and perhaps, cultural "adaptations" are not always necessary. A reasonable question, then, is "Can evidence of a program's effectiveness with a population that differs from its original intended recipients be used to argue that the program has cultural relevance?" The answer to this question may depend on how one defines true cultural relevance and what type of evidence is being used to argue the merits of a particular program. The question of whether using interventions designed for one population with a different cultural group produces positive outcomes has been examined on a larger scale by Wilson, Lipsey, and Soydan (2003). These authors conducted a meta-analysis examining whether delinquency prevention programs were effective for minority youth when compared with White youth. Their findings suggested that while positive effects were found for the main outcome variables in both ethnic groups, issues related to regular participation, acceptance of the program, and overall satisfaction were not equivalent. Are these latter outcomes as important as whether or not a program is successful in reducing targeted behaviors or symptoms? Additionally, one must wonder why would a program that is able to reduce symptoms be less acceptable or satisfying for ethnic minority participants? Both of these questions will be addressed in the remainder of this section.

One reason that a given set of prevention programs may evidence effectiveness but still lack cultural relevance is because the researchers may have failed to make meaningful efforts to increase the face validity of the program. As was previously discussed, deep-structure modifications (Resnicow et al., 2003) determine the cultural relevance of prevention programs. Often, the adaptations required for a prevention program to be truly culturally relevant result in a program that may be substantively different from its prototype (Reese & Vera, 2007). For example, a violence prevention program that taught participants to ignore the confrontations of instigating peers (e.g., walking away) may be inappropriate in a community where engaging in such behavior violates community norms of masculinity. However, a social justice orientation to prevention would necessitate that the participants have had an active voice in the prevention process from start to finish, which means that the face validity of the program, participants' satisfaction level and "buy in," and retention rates are just as important as whether traditional outcomes of effectiveness have been achieved.

Dryfoos (1990), Kenny and Romano (2009), Lerner (1995), Reiss and Price (1996), among others, have suggested that the most effective, culturally relevant prevention programs include the target program participants in the planning, implementation, and evaluation of the program. Furthermore, programs oriented toward social justice build on the strengths of the community and intervene with larger systems in addition to targeting interventions to the individual participants. When programs are successful in reducing symptoms but may not have succeeded in securing community "buy in," it is not surprising that one may find ambivalence about regular participation, overall satisfaction, or other indices of acceptance.

To illustrate, consider a college counseling center staff that is attempting to provide better services to promote the mental health of its gay, lesbian, bisexual, transgendered (GLBT) students. A culturally relevant program that includes participants in the planning, implementation, and evaluation phases of the program might begin by having an advisory committee that consists of GLBT students who can speak to the common and unique issues that they experience on the campus. The advisory committee would work collaboratively with the counseling center staff to develop initiatives that address social injustice issues, such as heterosexism, at either interpersonal or policy levels.

The committee might recommend that student leaders in the GLBT campus community be trained as para-professionals to participate in delivering some of the programs (e.g., organizing events to promote GLBT awareness on campus), whereas other types of programs would be delivered by counseling center staff (e.g., support groups on the coming out process). In addition to such interventions, the group may decide to advocate for the needs of GLBT students with university administrators (e.g., creating a GLBT student union that can serve as a safe place for the community). The evaluation of various programs might include both quantitative and qualitative feedback that is solicited by GLBT students as opposed to counseling center staff. This is just one example of how prevention program constituents would be involved in the prevention process from start to finish, which may result in a high level of buy in and investment in the outcomes of the efforts.

Thus, a "best practice" in the creation of culturally relevant, social justice–oriented prevention programs would be illustrated in authentic collaborations with the community, as has been illustrated in the aforementioned example. One issue that often comes up in working with marginalized communities, such as the GLBT community, is how do we know that our efforts have been successful and worthwhile? This question comes up in the context of any prevention program. However, in working with communities who have often been denied the same level of services that other groups have historically received, there can often be a negative reaction to administrators who, for example, want "proof" that the program can justify the allocation of resources. Hence, a discussion of program evaluation and social justice issues is warranted next.

Program Evaluation and Social Justice

The aforementioned discussion necessitates a conversation about what type of evidence we truly value in the field of prevention and how prevention programs that are culturally relevant and social justice oriented are best evaluated. One challenge for all such programs is found in providing sufficient evidence of success. Demonstrating a program's success is often critical to expanding a program and/or securing resources to support the program's continuation. Funders often want to know not only that a program has changed the participants in a positive way but that it has done so above and beyond what can be accomplished through alternative methods. For example, to secure funding for a culturally relevant, social justice–oriented approach to the prevention of sexually transmitted diseases, such as HIV, researchers may need to demonstrate that their program reduces incidents of such diseases and does so more effectively than a traditional sex education curriculum in a public school. Such criteria make sense in times when resources are finite and funding priorities must be defined.

Therefore, one important conversation that must accompany a review of research on the effectiveness prevention programs is how program evaluation is conceptualized. Traditional program evaluation prioritizes the use of scientifically rigorous clinical trials, often involving random assignment of participants to a program, and narrowly attempts to address the question "Did it work?" (Jacobs & Goldberg, 2009). Unfortunately, traditional ways of evaluating programs have also de-emphasized questions of participant satisfaction, social utility, or other more justice-oriented types of outcomes. These types of outcomes may give us valuable information about the interests of the participants or community members with whom we partner. Fortunately, advances in the field of program evaluation may reduce some of the tension historically experienced between protecting the interests of participants and protecting the interests of good science. In efforts to inform practitioners and policy makers about ways in which to accomplish this, Conyne (2010) has developed a 10-step prevention development and evaluation model that emphasizes community, collaboration, and cultural relevance. The model is based on rigorous research and includes specific evaluation steps.

As illustrated by the Conyne (2010) model, contemporary approaches to program evaluation are becoming much more flexible and pluralistic than traditional approaches (Jacobs & Goldberg, 2009). Rather than solely focusing on program outcomes, such as changes observed during and after the course of the intervention, more modern evaluation methods also value the program process or the ways in which programs are implemented, adapted, utilized, and retooled to respond to changes in the financial, political, or community arenas (Wight & Obasi, 2002). Jacobs and Goldberg (2009), Rosencrans et al. (2008), and Bledsoe and Graham (2005) all argue that attending to the processes of change within prevention programs ultimately yields improvements in design and implementation, as well as outcomes. Some of the following approaches to prevention program evaluation may represent philosophies to the task that are highly compatible with a social justice orientation. Note that consistent with the aforementioned definitions of social justice, these approaches also value both processes and outcomes of prevention efforts.

Empowerment evaluation, according to Bledsoe and Graham (2005) and Fetterman (1996), is a form of participatory evaluation (Upshur & Barreto-Cortez, 1995) that incorporates the perspectives of all those with a vested interest in a prevention program (i.e., stakeholders), usually those who are most invested in program development and the distribution of services. In short, empowerment evaluation allows for increased involvement of program stakeholders and allows them to identify and define those needs (and in what manner to evaluate those needs) that are most important to a program. This approach utilizes both qualitative and quantitative methodologies and seeks to highlight processes necessary for success.

Inclusive program evaluation is another type of evaluation meant not only to include stakeholders who have traditionally been recognized, such as funders, administrators, staff members, and participants, but also to seek out representation of members of groups who have been traditionally excluded from or misrepresented in the evaluation process (Mertens, 2003). The use of an inclusive approach encourages the development and use of qualitative measures, such as interviews, to provide rich data about the organizational and community context (Bledsoe & Graham, 2005). Often, these types of data allow for discussions about race, ethnicity, immigrant status, and socioeconomic status to elucidate how that diversity would influence the types of experiences consumers had in the program and the types of feedback generated. This approach can be useful in explaining how programs may be differentially effective for participants based on cultural backgrounds and past experiences of marginalization.

While these more contemporary approaches to program evaluation may be more consistent with the philosophy of prevention scholars, such as Lerner (1995), who argued that participants *must* have an active voice in the design, implementation, and evaluation of our prevention efforts if they are to be successful, there are still tensions that arise when different priorities emerge for various stakeholders in the process. For example, the need for randomized, control group program evaluation is stated as the sole criteria for prevention programs that would be eligible for federal grants (Biglan, Mrazek, Carnine, & Flay, 2003). However, oftentimes randomization and control groups, even if they are delayed-treatment control groups, are highly objectionable to community participants of prevention programs, especially in communities with few resources and significant problems to address (Reese & Vera, 2007).

To be truly consistent with the principles of social justice–oriented, culturally relevant prevention, one might opt to forego the use of random assignment and control groups in program evaluation if it is problematic for the program constituents and community members. However, such a decision may have significant scientific implications such as limiting the investigators' ability to speak confidently about the internal validity, or the extent to which the intervention actually caused the observed change, of their results should they find positive effects or secure funding for future. Being culturally responsive and scientifically rigorous are not necessarily incompatible goals, but when such conflicts arise, prevention scientists are often faced with difficult and important dilemmas. We believe that it is possible, however, to embrace and struggle with these challenges in a manner that allows the best interests of our constituents and science to be served.

Having flexible, community-oriented approaches to program evaluation creates opportunities for social justice–oriented prevention scientists not only to consider traditional outcomes of prevention program evaluation (e.g., formative and summative outcome data) but also to gather data that are meaningful to the sustainability of a program, to understand the ways in which the culture of the participants may be best reflected in program content, and to understand how perceptions based on cultural differences could affect the implementation of the program in the future (Bledsoe & Graham, 2005). We advocate a pluralistic approach to both program design and evaluation that utilizes methods reflecting processes consistent with social justice. In the following section of this book, we will discuss critical characteristics of culturally relevant social justice prevention programs and provide detailed examples of how these programs become established.

3

Application

Mechanisms for Creating Culturally Relevant, Social Justice–Oriented Prevention Programs

What should culturally relevant, social justice–oriented prevention look like and how is it established? We have seen one trend in the prevention field aimed at adapting established programs for use in communities that are different from the populations on which they were designed. While one could argue that implementing these programs in communities whose members are at greater "risk" for developing problems is a socially just endeavor, the kind of culturally relevant, social justice–oriented program we are advocating for involves preventionists doing far more than adapting traditional approaches to "nontraditional" communities. Rather, we believe that a "grassroots" approach, encouraged by Kenny and Romano (2009), Reiss and Price (1996), Lerner, Almerigi, Theokas, and Lerner (2005), Reese & Vera (2007), and others, will include the communities we aim to assist as true partners in the design, implementation, and evaluation of prevention programs. We also believe that broader skill sets are required in our efforts to be social justice oriented. Not only must we be able to work collaboratively with our participants, but we also must be able to serve as catalysts and advocates in addressing social injustices that are responsible for the perpetuation of particular problems in a community (Speight & Vera, 2008). Thus, we start our conversation about application, discussing the additional skill sets involved in being advocates.

Social justice–oriented prevention that is culturally relevant will often involve addressing larger systems that perpetuate injustices and disparities in a variety of mental health areas. Therefore, finding ways to intervene with these larger systems becomes a key objective of the program. In the spirit of this objective, prevention specialists can seek to orchestrate larger system change via community organizing, building political coalitions, and raising awareness of specific community problems with key constituent groups and decision makers (Cohen, Chávez, & Chehimi, 2007). These strategies move the prevention specialist outside the location of the service delivery to engage in outreach, collaboration, advocacy, community organizing, and social action–oriented research. These activities will be discussed next.

Although outreach, advocacy, collaboration, and activism are not exclusive to prevention, these strategies are important to advancing a social justice prevention agenda (Prilleltensky, 1997; Speight & Vera, 2008). Advocacy involves prevention professionals working with and/or on behalf of a community in challenging unjust institutional barriers and policies, and some activism-focused work involves direct efforts to reduce oppression and adverse social conditions (Chávez, Minkler, Wallerstein, & Spencer, 2007; Kenny & Hage, 2009). Dissemination of information to the public and policy makers, such as politicians, to increase awareness of systemic factors that foster injustice is an important strategy in social justice advocacy (Toporek, Lewis, & Crether, 2009).

Dissemination of information, in and of itself, may be insufficient to convince policy makers to take action, however, and it may also fail to capture public interest on a particular issue. Part of the reason for this is that there are often motivations to maintain the status quo, which have to do with protecting privilege. Specifically, many issues of social justice have financial implications about how limited resources might be distributed. If one group of constituents is asking for "more pie," it may mean that another group has to give up its pieces or make do with less pie. This scenario plays out in many states that fund their educational systems by using property tax income. Children who go to school in districts with higher property taxes, under this system, receive better educational resources than children who attend school in districts with lower property taxes. While the residents of higher tax districts may agree that it is unfair for children in lower tax districts to have poorer educational resources, they may be unwilling to sacrifice any of the resources that benefit their children to level the playing field.

As a result, it is often more than dissemination of information that is necessary to change social policy. Advocacy efforts also have to be accompanied by cost–benefit analyses that state the moral and financial benefit of addressing injustices. For example, it may be necessary to explicitly state the cost of *not* engaging in prevention efforts when communicating with politicians. If a politician can see how investing in a violence prevention program might ultimately save the taxpayers money by reducing the costs of incarcerating juvenile offenders, it may be more likely to garner that individual's support.

Fortunately over time, a variety of studies have addressed the cost–benefit ratios of prevention interventions and programs. These studies have calculated costs and benefits involved in alcohol use prevention (Kraemer, 2007), smoking cessation (Ruger & Emmons, 2008), and teen pregnancy prevention (Rosenthal et al., 2009). All of these studies provided convincing data that the economic benefits of prevention outweigh the financial costs. A landmark study of early intervention among African American children born in poverty demonstrated that it was more cost-effective to provide comprehensive pre-school intervention than to pay for prison later in life (Schweinhart et al., 2005). These children also had higher paying jobs, thus paying more taxes, than a comparison group. These data have been important over time in gar-nering public support for programs, such as Head Start. Hence, it is likely that data such as these will be important to provide to policy makers in any efforts to obtain their buy in.

In addition to policy advocacy, a variety of outreach efforts are aligned with social justice prevention. Outreach is most effective when prevention-ists join with community members to identify needs, assets, goals, and strategies to reach desired resources. The term *outreach scholarship* (Jensen, Hoagwood, & Trickett, 1999; Lerner & Overton, 2008) refers to collabora-tions between university researchers and community members that strive to advance knowledge of theory and research to build mutually beneficial and sustainable programs. Community-based participatory action research (PAR) is one type of outreach scholarship that gives voice to the community and contributes to social change (Arthur & Lalande, 2009; Cohen & Wolfe, 2007). PAR involves an ongoing process of collaborative planning, action, observation, reflection, evaluation, and change among all stakeholders for a shared purpose (Stringer, 2004).

As the following examples illustrate, outreach scholarship and PAR are very compatible with social justice–oriented prevention models. Fine and Torre (2006), for example, collaborated with prison inmates in the design and evaluation of a prison-based college program with the intent to affect public policy. By using data from prison records and the narratives of the inmates following release, the research team documented the positive impact of college study for the former inmates, their families, the community, and the state prison system. The social justice goal of the PAR project was to produce a document that was disseminated to the governor and state senators to con-tinue and expand financial support for the program. At the level of school change, Smith, Davis, and Bhowmik (2010) partnered with urban high school students who served as co-researchers in studying resources for health and sexuality education in the school setting. The findings, which were pre-sented by the students to school administrators, revealed an expressed need by students for classes related to sociocultural identity, substance abuse, rela-tional issues, and sexual health. A pilot program was developed as a result with the potential to promote wellness and prevent teen pregnancy and rela-tional and substance abuse. A PAR project developed in collaboration with racial minority parents of urban middle school students was designed to devise an inclusive definition of parental involvement and identify culturally relevant strategies for enhancing involvement (Snell, Nola, & East, 2009). The findings, which identified risk and protective factors and cultural values that impact how parents support their children and relate to school person-nel, were presented to school administrators and used to develop a program to improve communication between school staff and parents.

Direct attempts to alter social conditions and policies that create disproportionate risk for particular communities have been identified as an appropriate focus of social justice–oriented prevention. In the Best Practice
Guidelines on Prevention (Hage et al., 2007), prevention specialists are
encouraged "to engage in governmental, legislative and political advocacy
activities that enhance the health and well-being of the broader population
served" (p. 550). Not only have such efforts been critical as a best practice,
but attempts to influence policy development have also been successful in
affecting larger systemic factors (Speight & Vera, 2008). Citing the work of
Shore (1994) and Albee (1996), Hage et al. (2007) noted the historic social
justice impact of legislative accomplishments such as the desegregation of
schools and the reauthorization of the Individuals with Disabilities Act.
While the outcomes of these efforts may be much more long term in nature
than is typical for most prevention programming, the effects of such change
affect the well-being of individuals for generations to come.

Among the many social conditions that deserve the attention of prevention
professionals are equity and access to quality health care, education, and
employment, and the elimination of discrimination based on race and ethnicity, sex, social class, religion, spiritual background, and sexual orientation.
Although advocating for such changes is more political than not, it is important to note Prilleltensky's (2008) analysis of the ways in which power and
politics inevitably pervade research and practice in psychology. The mental
health field is not an objective and value-free field but rather has shaped
public policy over the years in both positive (e.g., *Brown vs. Board of
Education*, Affirmative Action; Buhin & Vera, 2009) and negative ways (e.g.,
using social science knowledge to fight national liberation movements around
the world during the 1960s; Prilleltensky, 2008).

In addition to interventions aimed at larger systems, culturally relevant,
social justice–oriented prevention must focus on developing the strengths of
community members, as has been discussed previously. Based on the resiliency literature (Masten, 2001), there are many developmental assets that
protect individuals from negative social conditions and other risk factors to
which they may be exposed. For example, having role models is important to
instilling self-efficacy and confidence in community members who may live
in contexts overrepresented by individuals who are under- or unemployed.
Instilling ethnic pride may be critical to enhancing well-being in communities
of color where discrimination and prejudice from others is commonplace
(Smith & Silva, 2011). Thus, in engaging in collaborative, democratic processes of program design and implementation, it is vital to incorporate objec-
tives that build capacity not only of individuals participating in the program
but also of the communities in which they live.

For example, Matthews, Pepper, and Lorah (2009) identified best practices
in promoting the mental health of GLBT students. They highlighted specific
programs that were offered within school settings (e.g., those that developed
alliances between straight and GLBT students), which evidenced effectiveness.

According to several program evaluation studies (Elze, 2003; Lee, 2002), it was revealed that programs that increased feelings of pride, confidence, and a sense of belonging in the school environment, in addition to those that increased feelings of safety by promoting advocacy efforts of teachers and administrators, were found to be most beneficial for participants. This is an example of how prevention programs that emphasize participants' strength building and advocacy with policy makers/school systems can be both culturally relevant and promote social justice.

Another example of a prevention program that aims at building strengths and influencing social conditions is the Young Warriors program developed by Watts (Watts, Abdul-Adil, & Pratt, 2002). The Young Warriors intervention cultivates critical consciousness and sociopolitical development in young African American men residing in low-income urban neighborhoods. The program developers also have created a community action project for the participants called "civic learning," which focuses on changing social systems. Participants in the Young Warriors program deconstruct and discuss rap videos and movies and use them as the point of departure for a wide range of topics on community change and development. When young men begin to take an interest in the sociopolitical dimension of their lives, acceptance and resignation give way to a growing awareness of and concerns about how inequality is established and maintained (Watts et al., 2002). The program evaluation of Young Warriors suggested that participants gain an increase in the frequency of critical thinking and increased willingness to take intellectual risks over the course of the program.

Finally, a key characteristic of culturally relevant, social justice–oriented prevention is the ability to truly partner with participating communities in the design, implementation, and evaluation of our efforts. Such partnerships allow for the "deep-structure" modifications that have been discussed throughout this text (Resnicow et al., 2003). A number of prominent scholars have followed these approaches in their design, implementation, and evaluation of prevention programs, several of which we will highlight next.

For example, Prilleltensky (Evans, Hanlin, & Prilleltensky, 2007) developed a model of collaboration between preventionists and participants that is strengths based and prevention, empowerment, and community focused (known as SPEC) to describe efforts that promote social justice. Their principles guide prevention efforts to be tailored to the specific goals of the community. Prilleltensky and colleagues have implemented this change process in health, human, and community service agencies through collaborative action research. Bess, Prilleltensky, Perkins, and Collins (2009), for example, applied the SPEC model in action-oriented work with community agencies to increase social justice values and to effect community empowerment and change.

Another set of guidelines for developing culturally relevant, social justice–oriented prevention programs is offered by Albee and Ryan-Finn (1993). These authors proposed a model that conceptualizes the emergence of mental health problems as a function of organic factors, stress, and environmental factors that foster oppression and inequity, all of which are offset by the strengths of the individual or group to resist the negative effects of oppression. According to this model, primary prevention should reduce the toxic environmental conditions (i.e., risk factors) while simultaneously fostering essential social change to reduce oppression, racism, and victimization and building assets that combat the effects of these forces.

Reaching Out About Depression (ROAD) represents an example of a grassroots mental health and community organizing project that was designed to build strengths, social support, and capacity among low-income women engaged in the welfare system (Banyard & Goodman, 2009). The program may be classified as tertiary prevention since many of the women entering the program already experience some psychological distress, with the program aiming to alleviate existing depressive symptoms and reducing risks that could lead to more serious difficulty. The program developed through the initiative of women who were threatened with a loss of welfare benefits, in collaboration with community activists and local academics. Through conversations, the women expressed feelings of being misunderstood by existing social and mental health services and described their current difficulties as a result of systemic factors at multiple ecological levels, including poverty, social isolation, and the experience of interpersonal violence. In line with Albee and Ryan-Finn's (1993) conceptualization of the incidence of mental health problems and the resiliency literature that emphasizes the protective value of social support (Masten, 2001), the program seeks to combat feelings of isolation and misunderstanding by building social support networks. The program also strives to recognize and enhance the strengths of the women and foster empowerment. A series of 12 Supportive Action Workshops are held with a focus on building social support and developing political and social advocacy skills so that the women can advocate and effect change in their lives. The workshops are facilitated by women who were the founding members of ROAD and former participants, who provide a capacity-enhancing peer network. A Resource Advocacy Team of psychology and law graduate students, referred to as partners, offer emotional and instrumental support to ROAD participants in response to acute crises where legal or psychological knowledge or support might be needed in responding to systemic injustice.

Keepin' it R.E.A.L, a school-based prevention program for youth in the Southwest (Gosin, Marsiglia & Hecht, 2003), is consistent with Albee's recommendations for enhancing resilience and reinforcing personal and cultural strengths. The program was developed to build resistance to the forces that lead to substance abuse by capitalizing on the strengths and cultural practices of youth in that community. For example, the curriculum created for Latino youth focused on the cultural values of *familismo* and *respeto* to help these adolescents make better choices, whereas a similar curriculum for African American youth was constructed around values of communalism and affective attunement to the needs of others. Both of these programs were successful in part because they were based on culturally relevant values for these adolescents rather than grounding the prevention program on European American values, such as individualism and objectivity. The program evaluation suggested that tailoring the curriculum to culturally relevant values helped the students actively engage in the activities and develop a personal connection to the materials covered in the lesson plans.

Romano and Netland (2008) discussed another model for integrating cultural norms and building on community strengths in a project that incorporated elicitation research as a process for including participants' cultural perspectives in the design of the intervention. Elicitation research's goal is to identify salient attitudes, relevant social norms, and beliefs about behavioral control from a population (Romano & Netland, 2008). This information is used to posit theories of what cultural strengths may be useful to promote in a prevention project (e.g., positive attitudes about the importance of education) and whether there are particular risk factors that may be appropriate to target for change (e.g., social norms supporting dropping out of school). They argue that using this approach from the inception allows preventionists to design programs that are culturally relevant and also target larger systemic variables (i.e., norms of the community or peer group). This approach may also be helpful in fostering culturally relevant deep-structure modifications in prevention design. While not specifically stated, it is possible that targeting systemic variables would include engaging in activities with a social justice orientation (e.g., political advocacy).

An illustration of the utility of the elicitation research process is found in the work of Koniak-Griffin et al. (2003) who designed an HIV/AIDS prevention program for low-income Latina adolescent mothers. By using elicitation research aimed at identifying knowledge about HIV, attitudes about prevention, and current risk-taking behaviors, Koniak-Griffin and colleagues developed a prevention program that targeted the specific needs, value systems, and behaviors of this group. The program also incorporated cultural beliefs on condom use, cultural norms on maternal protectiveness, and specific statistics on the devastating effects of HIV/AIDS on Latino communities. By making the program culturally relevant to the participants by including information germane to the gender and ethnic background of its participants, the researchers were able to personalize the content, which enhanced the change process and demonstrated positive outcomes such as greater knowledge of HIV/AIDS, higher intentions to use condoms, and fewer sex partners. Part of personalizing the content to the culture of the participants involved including issues that are more culturally relevant for Latina women such as conservative gender role ideologies that are promulgated by religion and the socialization of girls into more subservient roles in romantic, heterosexual relationships.

This section has elaborated on the three aspects of culturally relevant, social justice–oriented prevention: (1) it is based on collaborative relationships with participants who inform program design, implementation, and evaluation; (2) it addresses larger systems that put particular communities at risk via advocacy, policy work, and social action; and (3) it promotes the strengths of the participants/communities and emphasizes capacity building. To provide detailed examples of how such programs can be designed and implemented, we offer several case examples based on the work of the authors.

Case Study 1

This case involves the development of a prevention program with a high school that is experiencing low retention rates in its primarily Mexican American, low-income student population. The case was selected to illustrate issues of cultural relevance and social justice because it involves an educational disparity of social relevance, school dropout in low-income, ethnic minority populations, and the proposed interventions were aimed at affecting change at multiple levels of the system: individual, school, family, community, and public policy.

School dropout affects youth of all ethnic and racial groups, but it is particularly problematic for urban youth of color. An analysis of the most recent census data conducted by Hull House and Loyola University Chicago's Center for Urban Research and Learning (see http://www.luc.edu/curl/pdfs/mindingthegap1.pdf) concluded that Latino youth in the state of Illinois have the lowest graduation rates of any ethnic group. Thirty-seven percent of Latinos 25 years of age and older in metropolitan Chicago do not have a high school education. In Chicago's inner-city schools, it is not uncommon to see graduation rates of 40% for Latino boys and 60% for Latina girls (Harvard Civil Rights Project, 2004). Understanding the factors that may prevent Latino dropout is critical to developing strategies to combat the problem.

The first author's involvement with this school began several years ago when there was an opportunity to consult with the principal about the dropout problem at the school. At that time, a joint decision was made to begin examining this situation by conducting a fairly extensive needs assessment. The first step of the needs assessment involved identifying what factors were influencing students' intentions to stay in school. This was accomplished through surveying the entire freshman and sophomore student body. The needs assessment specifically targeted this population because previous research has determined that 9th and 10th grades are the years during which the most school dropout occurs (Harvard Civil Rights Project, 2004). If students make it to 11th grade, the likelihood of earning a diploma increases exponentially. Thus, we believed that capturing the perspectives of 9th and 10th graders would more likely depict the attitudes of both students who were at higher risk for dropping out and those who were more likely to graduate high school. The survey items were designed by incorporating existing measures found in the literature on factors significantly related to school retention: school belonging (Goodnenow, 1993), the availability of role models (Nakkula & Harris, 2005), social support networks (Vaux, 1988), achievement motivation (Goodenow & Grady, 1993), and academic self-efficacy (Midgley et al., 1997). We also included measures of factors that were predictive of school dropout: parental education, parental involvement in educational process, grade retention histories, home–school dissonance, and skepticism about the relevance of school (Midgley et al., 1997).

Participants in the survey were 1,194 students of Mexican American heritage, many of whom were from immigrant families, and while all the students enrolled in the 9th and 10th grades were eligible for participation with parental consent, of the 1,600 eligible, 75% chose to participate. The average age of the participants was 15.7 years and the gender breakdown was 49% boys and 51% girls. Ninety percent of the students qualify for free breakfasts/lunches, which indicates that their families live beneath the poverty line.

Survey Results

With regard to an examination of the descriptive data, girls, in general, had significantly higher mean scores on most of the measures, indicating more positive school experiences and attitudes than their male counterparts. In particular, girls had higher scores on achievement motivation than boys and indicated a higher likelihood of returning to school the following year. The only factors on which there were no such gender differences were on academic self-efficacy scores, parental involvement in school experience, and percentage of teachers that students like in the school.

As we expected, the vast majority of factors were highly intercorrelated, suggesting that students who, for example, had high academic self-efficacy also had a high sense of school belonging, high sense of relevance of their schoolwork to their future success, higher support from families and teachers, and so on. In examining which of all the possible factors would best predict students' intentions to return to school the following school year, we found that motivation achievement was the biggest predictor, accounting for 16.7% of the variance uniquely. School belonging and academic self-efficacy were also statistically significant predictors but together only raised the total percentage of variance accounted for to 19.7%. In terms of predicting academic aspirations, such as graduating high school, we found a similar result. Achievement motivation uniquely predicted 38% of the variance of academic aspirations. The perceived relevance of school to the future was also a significant predictor, as was academic self-efficacy, the presence of role models, and family support. However, these additional variables raised the total amount of variance explained to 42.8%. Students who had family members and other adults in their lives whom they admired, to whom they could go to for advice, and with whom they could share successes, along with having strong motivation to learn and master school subjects, were more likely to report high intentions to graduate high school and go on to college.

Moderation analyses revealed that with respect to intentions to return to school the next academic year, achievement motivation moderated the relationship between having repeated a grade and the outcome variable, as did self-efficacy. Two moderators were also found in examining the relationship between being behind in school credits and intentions to return to school: self-efficacy and total support. With respect to moderating academic aspirations and potential risk factors, four moderators were found to be significant: (1) achievement motivation moderated the relationship between perceived relevance of school to the future and academic aspirations; (2) academic self-efficacy moderated the relationship between repeating a grade and the outcome variable; and (3) total support and (4) academic self-efficacy moderated the relationship between being behind in credits and the outcome variable. The second part of the needs assessment involved communicating with the teachers about their perceptions of what puts certain students "at risk" for dropping out of school. We conducted a series of eight focus groups with approximately forty 9th- and 10th-grade teachers. The themes that emerged from these conversations were as follows:

- *Increasing efforts regarding classroom support:* Like many schools, this school faced challenges associated with large student-to-teacher ratios. Teachers spoke of the difficulties they experienced when students in the class required more specialized attention either due to their confusion with the subject material being presented or due to behavioral problems that warranted some type of adult intervention. The addition of qualified teacher assistants or aids in the classroom was identified as a key way that those students who may be at risk of school dropout or failure could receive the extra attention they need to keep pace with the other students in the class.
- *Increasing efforts regarding mentoring/role modeling:* While the current mentoring program used by the school was lauded by teachers, it was also stated that having a greater number and availability of mentors could be an excellent supplement to this retention mechanism. Potential sources of additional mentors included alumni, members of the community, and college students.
- *Increasing opportunities for students to earn field trips (and other educationally relevant privileges):* Teachers discussed the variety of experiences they have had using positive behavioral supports to increase the motivation of their students. While many felt that the idea had promise, there was some concern that there were too few incentives in place that were of real educational value to the students. Suggestions for incentives included field trips to plays, museums, or local college campuses as it was noted that many of the students had never visited such locations.
- *Increasing opportunities for extracurricular involvement:* To further increase students' feelings of engagement and belonging in the school,

teachers suggested that encouraging students and their families to participate in and attend school-sponsored events would be of value. The teachers acknowledged that there are a number of opportunities in place but that many of the freshman students were either not fully aware of what they were *or* were not allowed to participate by their families for a variety of reasons.

The information attained from both the student survey and the focus groups with teachers indicated that finding ways to increase the motivation of students, providing role models that might enhance their academic self-efficacy, and enhancing family support for academic involvement might be culturally relevant, participant informed, targets for intervention. One additional piece of anecdotal data that came from discussions with administrators was the fact that the school had a significant proportion of undocumented students enrolled, and there was some speculation that the current U.S. policies on higher education opportunities and job options for individuals who lacked legal documentation might serve as a deterrent for completing high school. While neither was this specifically addressed in the survey nor were teachers asked about the potential problem, according to school administrators, this often came up as the "elephant in the room" when strategizing ways to increase retention rates. Given that undocumented students are currently unable to secure federal financial assistance to attend college and that even with college degrees, such individuals are unable to obtain social security numbers that make them eligible for legitimate employment, it is not surprising that the academic motivation of such students may be difficult to improve.

Prevention Opportunities

In consultation with school administrators, there were several prevention opportunities identified to address school dropout in this community. First, introducing interventions that increased motivation for the students to stay in school was identified. This could be done in a variety of ways through the use of positive behavioral support systems (Koegel, Koegel, & Dunlap, 1996) tied to privileges or opportunities that could be earned through regular attendance and academic successes. Second, while the school had a mentoring program where 11th- and 12th-grade students served as role models to their 9th- and 10th-grade counterparts, it was clear that such a program could be expanded to include alumni and community members who might exemplify the connection between staying in school and career opportunities. By using alumni in a mentoring program, it would also serve the purpose of enhancing academic self-efficacy through vicarious means (Bandura, 1997), which would address another finding of the survey research we conducted. Third, it was also possible to design and deliver programs aimed at educating parents about the important role they play in the educational lives of their children. Some high schools have regular events for parents, sometimes referred to as "Parent University" during which such topics could be addressed. The school had a reputation for offering social events for families (e.g., mariachi nights to celebrate culturally significant events) but had yet to extend itself as a branch for educational opportunities such as English as a second language classes or psychoeducational topics. Enhancing family support, increasing motivation, and promoting self-efficacy were all strengths-based approaches to reducing rates of school dropout.

In addition to interventions aimed at the school community specifically, it also was important to examine public policy that may not promote high school graduation in Latino students. One specific policy that is socially relevant and timely is the DREAM Act, which was recently approved in 2011 by the U.S. House of Representatives but was ultimately defeated by the Senate. This federal policy would make it possible for adolescents who came to the United States illegally as children to apply for citizenship if they either enrolled in the military or attended college after high school graduation. While there is some controversy surrounding this policy, there is also an argument to be made for the societal consequences of having a significant number of high school dropouts in a community. Among the correlates of dropping out of high school are the aforementioned limited vocational opportunities (De la Rosa & Maw, 1990), criminal activity (Harlow, 2003), teenage pregnancy (Coley & Chase-Lansdale, 1998), and other risky behaviors. Thus, another prevention opportunity would be advocacy at the federal level to support legislation such as the DREAM Act, if and when it is reintroduced for enactment.

On a related level, there were also opportunities to meet with state elected officials who developed educational policies. The first author had in the past presented testimony to the educational caucus of the state legislature specifically trying to raise awareness of the specific issues influencing Latino students. While this type of advocacy may require longer-term commitment than would some of the school-specific types of prevention activities, it is socially just to engage in efforts that may in the long run accomplish feats that more short-term efforts would be unable to affect. Attending to the political climate that surrounded educational achievement for this particular cultural group is an example of how prevention efforts can target larger social conditions that create disproportionate risk for particular communities.

In terms of evaluation, we plan to adopt a pluralistic approach to determine the success of our efforts. Clearly, one way to determine our success is to track the retention and graduation rates of students who participated in our efforts. Second, we are very interested in how the program is perceived by students, teachers, parents, and administrators. The best way to obtain this information may be to conduct focus groups and interviews at different points throughout the process to get formative feedback about our efforts and how they might be fine-tuned to best meet the evolving needs of the community. Tracking the success of our policy advocacy efforts is more challenging in that the political climate and financial status of the state in which this program was offered, and the country in general, may not favor an immediate adoption of the DREAM Act or an allocation of funds aimed at Latinos specifically. However, in the long term, it is hoped that there will be some change in the political climate that surrounds school achievement for Latino communities.

Case Study 2

Our second case example also evolved through collaborations between university faculty and administrators and two urban public high schools. As in the first case example, the intervention that developed through these collaborations is designed to prevent school dropout and promote school engagement. Recent data reveals that in many urban school districts, half or more of students in the ninth grade do not stay in school to completion of their high school diplomas (MacIver & MacIver, 2010). The program described in this case is designed to be preventive not only by reducing risks but also by building strengths among the students, the schools, families, and communities. In this way, the intervention is consistent with a focus on fostering positive youth development (Catalano, Berglund, Ryan, Lonczak, & Hawkins, 2002; Lerner, 2001; Pittman, Irby, Tolman, Yohalem, & Ferber, 2001). Our intent was not only to reduce school dropout but also to maximize the capacities of youth to thrive and be fully prepared for life and work. Advanced academic and critical thinking skills are increasingly essential for success in the workplace and engagement in the political process (Cochran-Smith, Gleeson, & Mitchell, 2010; Jerald, 2009). To the extent that work is a means not only for economic survival but also as a source of power, social connection, and self-determination (Blustein, Kenna, Gil, & Devoy, 2008), efforts to enhance school engagement and career planning of youth are integral for advancing social justice.

School Context

These urban public schools, as is characteristic of many public schools in large urban settings in the United States, are underresourced in comparison with public schools in more affluent suburbs and are confronted with myriad challenges associated with the economic poverty that is often present in the communities in which they are nested (Balfanz, 2009). The student populations of the two high schools that are part of these collaborations are ethnically and racially diverse (60% Black/African American and 30% Latino/a) according to school records (Kenny & Bledsoe, 2005). While it is important to emphasize that many members of diverse racial and ethnic groups enjoy middle-class and higher levels of income (Reese & Vera, 2007), more than 70% of students in this district as a whole qualify for free or reduced-price lunch, and 30% live in poverty based on U.S. census data (Sum, 2008). For the past decade, the dropout rate for students attending the city public schools has hovered around 20%, with a disproportionate number of dropouts being students of color, particularly young males (Sum, 2008). Furthermore, there has been a large gap between the percentage of White high school graduates from the city schools who go on to attend and complete college in comparison with the Black and Latino high school graduates (Sum, 2008).

Moreover, this city is the home of a large number of colleges and universities, with the population of students attending the public schools contrasting with the generally White and more affluent student and young professional population of the city. While 2010 community survey data (U.S. Census Bureau) reveal that 60% of the city residents were White and 15% received food stamps/SNAP (Supplemental Nutrition Assistance Program) benefits, just 13% of students attending the city public schools were White and 76% qualified for free or reduced-price lunch. Social inequities are clear when the cultural, intellectual, and economic resources of the city's institutions and young professional population are compared with the limited access to these resources available to low-income families whose children attend the city's schools. Collaborations between universities and public schools have the potential to enhance social justice by extending the intellectual and financial resources of the university to the communities (Kenny, Sparks, & Jackson, 2007). A long history of collaboration between our university and two public high schools in closest proximity to the university developed in efforts to address these inequities. In recognition of the strengths of the schools and communities with which we have partnered, it is critical to acknowledge the reciprocal benefits of these relationships and the extent to which our partnerships with the schools enrich our learning and that of the university students. The program described in this case example is part of a broader and constantly evolving system of collaborations existing between the university and these two schools, and with other community organizations located in the urban center surrounding the university.

The program is a universal primary prevention program designed to promote self, community, and career awareness and student understanding of the relationship between success in school and in career (Kenny, Sparks, et al., 2007; Solberg, Howard, Blustein, & Close, 2002). The program includes a psychoeducational curriculum that is delivered to all ninth-grade students in the two schools and is preventive in its efforts to prevent dropout and promote academic engagement. The program is delivered in the classroom for one class period per week across the academic year. The 30 weekly class sessions include activities and exercises designed to enhance self-knowledge; clarify career and educational goals; identify personal, cultural, and community strengths; consider barriers to the achievement of educational and career goals; and increase motivation to pursue those goals by emphasizing the linkages between school and work. In addition to activities in the classroom, students also visit the university setting; meet with current students, including graduates of their own high school; tour the campus; and meet with admissions and financial aid staff, as a means for helping students visualize themselves in the college setting and to increase knowledge for navigating the pathways through high school to college. Although these activities inevitably reduce time in class devoted to traditional academic instruction, the program addressed this in two ways. First of all, the program was developed based on evidence that student motivation and engagement in school are central to academic achievement and can be facilitated by the presence of academic and career goals (Kenny, Blustein, Haase, Jackson, & Perry, 2006; Lapan, 2004). Second, an academic literacy-building exercise was included in many of the lessons, so that students applied academic skills to college exploration and career development activities.

As we will explain, the program developed and evolved over time in ways that are consistent with the principles for social justice and culturally relevant collaborative relationships we have set forth in this book and, in other ways, have struggled to fully meet these ideals. The following program description focuses on the role of collaboration in program design, implementation, and evaluation.

Collaboration in Program Design

The initial impetus for the primary prevention program described in this case example grew out of a prior collaboration between one of the university faculty and the school-to-career coordinator at one of the two high schools that resulted in a school-based homework completion program (Kenny, Sparks, et al., 2007). Their review of the effectiveness and limitations of the school-based homework intervention stimulated discussion concerning further and potentially more effective collaborations between the university and the school-to-career office at the district level. The high school coordinator discussed possibilities for university collaboration with the district representatives, who expressed a strong interest in further engagement with the university faculty and noted that there was an excellent fit between their agenda and the interests and scholarly expertise of the faculty. Both the school district leaders and the university faculty believed that helping young people understand the connection between school and work and linking learning at school with activities in the workplace would enhance school engagement (Blustein, Juntunen, & Worthington, 2000; Kenny, Gualdron, et al., 2007). A top-down endorsement for the project was thus obtained, along with involvement of the central office in the initial planning and financial support of the project. Although an initial endorsement of a project at the school district level is in some way contrary to social justice principles, whereby program development grows out of community voice (Fondacaro & Weinberg, 2002), "buy-in" at the district level was critical in advancing the development of this project. Collaborations with public school systems inevitably involve the navigation of school bureaucracy. The support we garnered at the district level allowed us to engage interest and attention from collaborators at the school level. We then had to build trust and mutually beneficial collaborative relationships with our school-based partners. The central office identified two high schools as ideal for the development of a school-to-career intervention based on the staff and structures present at each school for delivering the curriculum and the presence of newly formed parent and community councils with whom to collaborate.

At the school level, one of the first steps in our collaboration was to meet with the school administrators, teachers, and staff. We engaged in a needs assessment and planning process with teachers, school counselors, and school-to-work coordinators from each school over a 4-month period. Payment to high school teachers and school staff for work during the summer and beyond the school day was available from the funding provided by the school district office and through a small grant that the university collaborators secured through their university. We found that having some funds to compensate teachers and school staff is critical in solidifying commitment and communicating respect for their time and professional expertise. With these partners, we planned and carried out focus groups with other teachers and staff at both schools that informed our understanding of the perceived school and student needs, provided suggestions for program content and mechanisms for program delivery, and increased our knowledge of the cultural and social context of the school and the student body. Collaboration among mental health professionals, teachers, administrators, and school counselors brings a number of voices to the table, with varied perspectives, that offer an opportunity to develop a strengths-based focus that emphasizes student, family, community, and cultural assets.

Our efforts to reach out to the parent councils at both schools were somewhat less successful. Although we also had some funding to compensate parents, issues of work, child care, transportation, and the general complexities of their lives appeared to limit the extent of family involvement in this process. The parent council that was in development at one of the schools failed to materialize for these reasons, we were told. Collaboration with families requires considerable effort in reaching out to find times beyond the school day and places to meet that accommodate the realities of their lives. It is plausible as well that families did not participate more actively in the school-based programs because they did not view the programs as culturally relevant, were not invested in them, or did not have the time and energy beyond their work and family caregiving responsibilities. This would be an important area for collaborative investigation prior to further program development or replication. In our case, the impetus for the intervention emerged from school and university concerns and not from the families or students themselves. The students from the high schools were involved in the planning and program development process to the extent that this was possible based on their schedules and availability. We were able to engage student participation when meetings were held at the school and during school hours. Finding times when teachers, students, and administrators were all free to meet during the school day was difficult, however, and additional financial compensation could only be offered to teachers in after-school hours due to union regulations.

Collaboration in Program Implementation

The program was implemented collaboratively by university faculty, graduate students in mental health counseling, school counseling, and counseling psychology and classroom teachers, with additional support from the school counselor and school-to-work coordinator at each school and recent graduates of the high schools. A team-teaching model for implementation was important, but it presented its own challenges. To facilitate interprofessional collaboration and cultural relevance and competence, ongoing training and supervision were needed.

The faculty and graduate students in mental health and counseling generally had little experience in high school teaching. The teachers at the high school shared knowledge and expertise in pedagogical practice, classroom organization and management, and ways to engage students in active learning. Since the program was delivered as a psychoeducational intervention for a class of 25 to 30 high school students, the skills offered by the teachers were critical. For graduate students in mental health and counseling to increase their pedagogical and classroom management skills, we also enlisted consultation and training from doctoral students enrolled in the university Curriculum and Instruction program. Since many of the counseling graduate students were novices in delivering preventive interventions, especially with young people who differed from them culturally, racially, and socioeconomically, the university faculty held weekly group supervision sessions to train and support the students for this work. These were supplemented by additional workshops related to cultural competence, curriculum development, and group process. These were open to both the graduate students and teacher cofacilitators and were taught by university faculty, with expertise in multiculturalism and racial identity. Graduates of the two high schools who now attended the local university were also invited to contribute to the facilitator workshops, to lend a local perspective to the curriculum development, to participate in sessions for students at the school and at the university, and to offer feedback for enhancing the cultural relevance of the program. We recognized, however, that the perspectives of the urban high school graduates may now be somewhat transformed as a result of their college experience. Workshops for facilitators were held both at the university and in the school setting and provided an opportunity for educators and mental health professionals to share experiences and insights and to revise the intervention collaboratively.

While the process of interprofessional collaboration served to expand the teachers and mental health professionals' mutual understanding of the students, the perspectives of the two professions were sometimes at odds and had to be reconciled. For example, one teacher was concerned that all students participate in every class discussion and felt that the counseling perspective, which viewed the sharing of personal information as voluntary, was not fair to all students. The teacher and counselor had to decide and set guidelines together for the kinds of student participation that would be voluntary and mandatory. It is our experience that the collaborative process of implementation enriched the intervention, but it was also time-consuming and required ongoing attention.

Collaboration in Evaluation

A scientist–practitioner approach to prevention includes grounding the work in existing theory, research, and ongoing evaluation of the program. We sought to follow sound practice in prevention (Hage et al., 2007; Walsh, DePaul, & Park-Taylor, 2009) and base the intervention in established theory and research. Career development (Blustein et al., 2000), racial and ethnic identity (Helms, 1990; Phinney, 1993), and developmental–contextual theories (Vondracek, Lerner, & Schulenberg, 1986) and research were centrally integrated in the conceptualization and delivery of the intervention. Related theoretical concepts and research were shared and discussed among all collaborators to constantly assess the validity and cultural relevance of the premises derived from the scholarly literature for our setting. We debated, for example, the extent to which the academic and career planning focus of our intervention was culturally relevant and conducted a study to further explore the meaning of work for the students (Chaves et al., 2004). School-based collaborators also expressed concern that evaluation questions posed to students that inquired about the employment and educational background of their family members would be perceived by students as culturally insensitive or intrusive, especially if family members did not have legal status in the United States. Feedback from the school-based collaborators suggested that they enjoyed the exposure to and discussion of relevant theory and research. We found dialogue with school-based collaborators extremely useful in challenging our preconceived notions of urban education and youth.

As we discussed in the research section of this book, research and program evaluation can be challenging from a social justice and cultural relevance perspective. With this awareness, we sought to follow a Development-in-Context-Evaluation (DICE; Ostrom, Lerner, & Freel, 1995) approach. This approach includes both process and outcome evaluation and includes multiple types of data from multiple sources over time. The findings from one phase of the evaluation are used to modify or adapt the intervention in efforts to enhance its cultural relevance, progress in attaining social justice goals, and overall effectiveness.

Our evaluation approach, similar to Case Study 1, included the use of standardized measures with students to assess over time relevant psychological constructs, such as school identification (Voelkl, 1997), social support (Cutrona & Russell, 1987; Harter, 1985; Taylor, Casten, & Flinkinger, 1993), ethnic identity (Phinney, 1993), and indices of career development and outcome expectations (McWhirter, Rasheed, & Crothers, 2000; O'Brien, 1992; Super, Thompson, Lindeman, Jordaan, & Myers, 1981). The quantitative measures were useful in providing baseline data for our sample and in assessing the validity of some of the assumptions underlying the intervention. For example, our findings affirmed our assumptions about the relationship between career awareness, career exploration, and school engagement (Kenny et al., 2006). Our research also supported programmatic assumptions about the value of relational support from teachers, peers, and family members (Kenny & Bledsoe, 2005; Kenny, Blustein, Chaves, Grossman, & Gallagher, 2003) and the challenges presented to school engagement and career development as a function of contextual barriers (Kenny et al., 2003; Kenny, Gualdron, et al., 2007).

With regard to formative assessment, student perceptions of program relevance, helpfulness, and perceived resources and barriers were assessed through open-ended questionnaires, focus groups, and individual interviews. Individual interviews and focus groups were also completed with teachers and school staff. The feedback from students, teachers, and school staff identified the strengths of the program, as well as areas for improvement that we then sought to address in program revisions. Family members were not engaged in program evaluation. As discussed with regard to program development, the school-based parent center had closed, and we did not devise a new strategy for reaching out to families at this stage of the intervention. With regard to student outcomes, high school graduation data and grades were obtained from school records and a subsample of students were interviewed at the time of high school graduation to learn more about their post–high school plans and the meaning they gave at this point in their lives to the ninth-grade intervention. Those interviews suggested that those students who participated in our program, along with other programs to support college readiness and enrollment, had developed and followed through with plans for entering higher education.

While our overall evaluation approach, with attention to process evaluation, proved helpful in identifying areas for program modification, the outcome evaluation was limited in its capacity to assess effectiveness according to scientific standards. Random assignment was not possible, and our evaluation did not include a control group. Modification of the program from year to year with different cohorts, as informed by formative evaluation, contributed to an intervention that lacked standardization. Because the evaluation was taking place in a broader context of social, economic, and political change that affected the structure and funding of the schools and economic opportunities related to employment and financial aid for higher education, it was difficult to separate the impact of the evaluation and broader social change. Additionally, some of the indices, such as records of school dropouts, that might be assumed ecologically valid indices of program effects were unreliable as the schools could not ascertain with confidence whether students were actually dropouts or whether they moved to another school. Thus, what we believe would be the strongest evidence, such as school grades and high school completion, to support our program effects did not yield significant findings.

Throughout the evaluation, we were concerned about the cultural relevance of our program and whether the program reflected culture at a deep-structure or superficial level (Resnicow et al., 2003). For example, we sought to incorporate music, art, and film in our intervention, which were popular among the students attending these schools, and to include literature that is drawn from lists of culturally relevant readings for this age-group. We wondered, however, whether these efforts were superficial and whether central constructs and premises of our intervention related to the connection between school and work resonated with the cultural belief systems of the students. We struggled in our initial efforts, especially in the classroom groups co-led by White, middle-class graduate students and faculty, to facilitate discussions related to racial and social class barriers and strategies for circumventing those barriers. Interviews with high school participants about racial barriers and discussions among consulting faculty and graduate students with particular expertise in the promotion of culture and racial identify were helpful, we believe, in our efforts to move toward the integration of racially relevant constructs at a deep-structure level (Blustein et al., 2010; Kenny, Gualdron, et al., 2007). As our intervention became more sophisticated in promoting critical consciousness or an understanding of the systemic causes for social and economic inequity related to race and ethnicity (Freire, 1972; Watts et al., 2002), we also confronted challenges as some public school teachers were not comfortable with the integration of social critique into public school class discussion. We debated how to introduce the discussion of racism into public school classrooms in ways that did not place undue responsibility on students to effect social change and individually navigate racial barriers. Although some teacher education programs prepare preservice teachers with an understanding of critical race theory (Cochran-Smith, 2000; Delgado & Stefanic, 2001), which recognizes the role of institutionalized racism in contributing to group advantage and disadvantage, most practicing teachers are unfamiliar with methods to effectively integrate social critique into classroom discussion and to challenge institutionalized racism within school and classroom policies and practices (Mitchell, 2011). Since these topics are not typically discussed in teacher education or in the public high school class setting, teachers were reluctant to raise issues and stir feelings that we would have inadequate time to process or resolve within the time constraints of our weekly classroom intervention. The preparation and cultural competence of both the counselors and teachers facilitating the intervention inevitably contribute to variation in the extent to which prevention is culturally relevant and transformative in a social justice sense.

With regard to outcomes, we were also concerned about whether the intervention, consistent with social justice principles, effected social change beyond the individual at multiple system levels. As previously mentioned, our involvement with families was limited, and hence our impact at that level was not assessed. In the absence of direct opportunities to meet with family members, we attempted to communicate with families through school newsletters and teacher–family nights at the school. We also intentionally designed some program activities to include family interaction. For example, students were asked to interview an extended family member or close family friend about the meaning of work in their lives; the personal, familial, and community resources they had drawn on; and how they had navigated barriers they had encountered (Kenny, Bower, Perry, Blustein, & Amtzis, 2004). This assignment yielded rich reports from many students and comments that these were insightful conversations that they had not had before.

We observed evidence of some change at the classroom level. As a result of the classroom discussions, the teachers with whom we worked expressed increased awareness of the impact of contextual challenges and obstacles in the lives of their students (Kenny, Gualdron, et al., 2007). Given the isolation experienced by some teachers in instructing and managing students in the classroom, the opportunity to work collaboratively with university graduate students and faculty offered intellectual stimulation and emotional support that several teachers described as revitalizing. Although school principals were involved in discussion regarding the development and implementation of the program, we did not have evidence that our intervention affected schoolwide policies or practices at the time of the intervention.

The faculty who were involved in the development, implementation, and evaluation of the classroom-based intervention became involved in social and political action and systemic change that grew out of this work. For example, our connection with the district-level leaders contributed to contacts for one faculty with leaders in the State Department of Education and involvement of the faculty member on a committee that developed policy and guidelines for career education at the state level. Another faculty member was appointed to a school district– and city-level committee involved in the reorganization and restructuring of several city high schools, including one of the intervention schools. Through this committee, the faculty member worked with families, community agencies, and business and civic leaders in developing the school vision, selecting school leadership, and designing educational and work-based learning opportunities for students who were consistent with social justice ideals. In this way, involvement in prevention at one level contributed to opportunities for involvement in social change at a broader level.

Systemic Change

Despite our efforts to effect contextual change, systemic issues beyond our control influenced the course of our intervention and its outcomes. For example, the economic downturn of the past several years inevitably affected students' perceptions of future opportunities and the extent to which their efforts at school will result in rewarding employment opportunities. Our efforts to emphasize student and community strengths and to facilitate the empowerment of students to navigate the challenges in their schools and communities become more difficult when external barriers to success are great. Despite these barriers, we recognize the importance of assisting students in developing the skills that empower them to overcome adversities present in their schools, communities, and the society at large (Vera, 2007). While our university–public school collaborations have sought to enhance the resources of the schools, the economic downturn also reduced school budgets and has a demoralizing impact on teachers and school administrators, who are being held increasingly responsible for the test scores of their students, irrespective of the negative impact of broad social conditions (Darling-Hammond, 2006).

If prevention programs are to have long-lasting social justice effects, they need to be sustainable and not depend on university connections or unreliable sources of grant funding (Walsh et al., 2009). This program evolved through impermanent sources of governmental and university funding. With this in mind, we sought to follow the prevention and social justice principle of "giving tools" to both the students and the teachers (Goodman et al., 2004). In our work with the teachers and involvement in the school restructuring efforts, we sought to identify and build teacher capacity and institutional support for continuing this work through advisories and other school-based structures, such as train-the-trainer models, that do not rely on the continuing presence of university faculty and graduate students. Budget cuts, along with the pressures on teachers to raise test scores, and declining support for interventions other than direct academic instruction have threatened these efforts in the absence of definitive data from scientifically valid studies to affirm the impact of the intervention on test scores or school dropout rates.

Over a 5-year period, this prevention program was delivered to more than 1,500 students across the two schools. This work continues at present in the context of a positive youth development program that fosters college entry among students at the same two partnering high schools (Blustein et al., 2012). The curriculum that was developed for use with all ninth-grade students is now delivered among a smaller group of students in after-school, summer, and Saturday programs. Although the current configuration of the program remains limited in its capacity to effect broad social change, at least in the short term, it subscribes to social justice goals in its intent to provide youth with critical skills that are essential to full participation in a democratic society. The collaborative youth development program representing a partnership between the university and high schools has existed for many years but was revised in recent years to build student academic skill in the context of social action projects. For example, groups of students identify a problem of concern to them in their school or community, complete field-based research and a review of existing literature related to the problem, and develop an action plan that is presented to multiple audiences at their schools, communities, and university. This initiative, similar to programs launched through organizations, such as Teaching to Change LA and Just Schools California, sought to empower youth by developing critical knowledge and tools to effect social change through action research (Rogers, Morrell, & Enyedy, 2007). We also viewed this as a means for building academic skills and an understanding of the value of these skills in a format other than traditional academic instruction.

With funding from the National Science Foundation, the youth development program now seeks to develop student interests and skills in science and technology through action research (Blustein et al., 2012). The preventive intervention as it was delivered within the schools is coupled with a program that teaches science and technology skills. The university faculty in science education and counseling psychology partner with the high school science teachers and school counselors in program development and delivery. Students are taught to use advanced technologies to study urban ecology and to analyze their findings through a social justice lens. For example, students have learned how to use GIS (Geographic Information System) technology to evaluate the impact of tree density on temperature and pollution in the urban environment. Social justice issues become clear to the youth as they identify and analyze which neighborhoods and income areas have the highest density of greenery within the city limits and the relationships of greenery with the ecological quality. Given the growing importance of basic and advanced skills in science and technology for entry into advancement in the workplace of the 21st century (Partnership for 21st Century Skills, 2008), equipping youth with technological skills along with an understanding of the practical, social justice, and career value of these skills is intended to enhance school engagement, academic efficacy, and career entry in STEM (Science, Technology, Engineering, and Mathematics) fields. The social justice implications of this are great when the economic advantages of STEM training and the underrepresentation of students of color in STEM studies and industries are considered (Blustein et al., 2012; National Science Board, 2008). Although the long-term outcomes have not yet been examined, the program appears to sustain and consolidate high school students' interests in STEM studies and careers across a development period when they otherwise might be discouraged. The students affirm positive racial identities and do not perceive their race or gender as obstacles to their educational and career development (Blustein et al., 2012).

From a social justice perspective, this case study illustrates the role of collaboration in prevention and the challenges in engaging all stakeholders in that process. The relevance of multiple ecological levels, including the person, family, school, community, state, nation, and global community, for program impact is considered. The importance of systemic change and of recognizing strengths and empowering individuals and communities as a means for promoting social justice are recognized.

Summary

This volume has provided a rationale for social justice and culturally relevant prevention and has presented principles of theory, research, and practice that inform this work. Detailed case examples have been offered to illustrate the development, implementation, and evaluation of prevention programs from the perspectives of social justice and cultural relevance. The cases also reveal the challenges of this work. We summarize some of these issues highlighted in this volume before asking you to apply them to learning exercises.

Although primary prevention is aligned with a social justice perspective because it aims to reduce human suffering before it occurs, all prevention activity does not realize the goals of social justice. Consistent with the perspective of George Albee (2000), we argue that to promote social justice, prevention should seek to reduce the social conditions, such as social oppression and inequality, that contribute to societal disparities in health, education, and psychological well-being. Also consistent with the work of Albee (Albee & Ryan-Finn, 1993) and Prilleltensky (Prilleltensky, Dokecki, Frieden, & Wang, 2007), we argue that in addition to targeting social equalities, social justice prevention should strive to build the capacity for all individuals and groups to participate fully in all aspects of society, to foster equity in social and political power, and to promote strengths and coping skills for responding to societal stress and oppression. Social justice outcomes include the reduction of risks and the enhancement of strengths at multiple levels, ranging from the person to the family, school, community, and broader social structures and policies.

For the above social justice outcomes to be facilitated, social justice prevention must also attend to processes that respect and build social and political equity across program design, implementation, and evaluation. We argue that collaboration is an essential aspect of prevention that seeks to foster social justice. Health and educational disparities in the United States are most prevalent for those who have been traditionally excluded from full societal participation, including the poor, people of color, the unemployed, the elderly, disabled, women, gay men, lesbians, and bisexual people. It is essential therefore that these persons be given voice in the development of prevention programs. Collaboration is a means not only for empowerment but also for creating conditions that enhance the success of prevention efforts. Collaboration that gives an active voice to persons of color, for example, is critical for the development, implementation, and evaluation of programs that are culturally relevant and thus meaningful for participants. Cultural relevance that is achieved at a deep-structure, rather than superficial, level can enhance recruitment, sustained participation, and prevention program outcomes. Unfortunately, minor adaptations in existing programs to make them appear culturally relevant are much more common that deep-structure modifications.

To achieve social justice and culturally relevant prevention, we have identified some of the skills and practices that can be applied toward this goal. Beyond the development of multicultural competence, prevention practitioners need to be equipped with skills in outreach, advocacy, and collaboration. Since traditional program evaluation can be limited in including the voice of all stakeholders, in being responsive to the need for change in response to formative evaluation, and documenting program effects, alternative evaluation models, such as empowerment evaluation, inclusive program evaluation, PAR, and elicitation research, should be considered. Because the findings of research and program evaluation can be used to effect system change, prevention practitioners need to develop skills and make time for disseminating their findings to public and policymakers.

Most prevention initiatives do not have the capacity to effect change across all levels. Nevertheless, much prevention work remains focused at the person level. We urge you to consider ways for fostering social change at the school, community, institutional, and public policy levels.

4

Learning Exercises

The following learning exercises are intended to help you apply what you have learned about social justice issues and culturally relevant prevention in a "real-world" context. Each of these exercises represents actual situations that we have encountered in our own prevention efforts.

Learning Exercise 1: In the Name of Science

You have been conducting a social and emotional skill-building program in an underresourced school community for several years now. The school does not have the resources for a full-time mental health professional, so the only children who typically are seen by the part-time social worker are those who are in crisis. As a prevention scientist, you have a commitment to providing interventions that are empirically supported and theoretically sound. You approach the school administrators about being able to begin a more formal evaluation of your program. As one aspect of this program evaluation, you would like to create a comparison group of children who would either not receive the program or who would receive the program at a later date (a delayed-treatment control group). When you discuss your ideas with the school administrator, she says,

> This program is so great and it gives our kids information and help that they don't get anywhere else. We *know* that this program helps, so I don't understand why you want to keep some of our kids from being able to participate.

Clearly, this administrator is thinking about the needs of her students more than the importance of program evaluation. How would you respond to her statement? In small groups or with a partner, attempt to debate this issue of what type of program evaluation is justifiable. Would you attempt to convince her that the program's evaluation is more important than making sure that every child is able to participate at the same time? Why or why not? Given what you have read about the variety of ways in which programs can be evaluated, are there any compromises that you can come up with that might please both the prevention scientist and the school administrator?

_____ Learning Exercise 2: Be Prepared

You are delivering a prevention program in a community where there are chronic problems with community violence. After a detailed needs assessment, you have decided to focus on helping participants learn to identify and avoid potentially dangerous situations and have a curriculum in place that will require eight sessions from start to finish. In the middle of the program, after your fourth session, you arrive at the community center and find many of the center staff in tears. They inform you that one of your participants, an 11-year-old boy, has been shot over the weekend in gang-related violence and is laying in a coma, fighting for his life. While some of the participants are aware of this state of affairs, others still have not been informed. The community center staff ask if you, as a mental health professional, would be willing to inform the program participants about what has happened and, then, offer some type of support and/or counseling to them given the current crisis. You and your program staff had come prepared to offer a module on safe, supervised, community recreation opportunities. You had no prior knowledge of what had happened over the weekend. At this point, there are about 30 minutes before program participants begin arriving at the center. You must now discuss quickly with your staff what to do, given the new state of affairs. Assuming that there are going to be some risks of either addressing the issue directly in lieu of what you had planned for the program that day _or_ failing to address the issue altogether, talk with a partner about how you would go about deciding whether it is better to go with what you have planned or to agree to the request of the community center staff. Imagine you decide to address the incident. What issues would you talk about as part of this discussion? Imagine you decide that it is better to stick with what has been prepared as part of the program. What might be the justification for moving forward with the plan? What decision would you ultimately make?

_____ Learning Exercise 3: Community Organizing?

You are working with a local elementary school on preventing school dropout. The community is largely made up of immigrants, some of whom are in the United States without legal documentation. As part of the program, you work with teachers and other school staff to educate them about some of the factors related to school dropout in this population.

One of the issues you discuss with them is the problem facing undocumented children with regard to higher education and, ultimately, employment, as their legal status will prevent them from being able to get a social security card, obtain government support for school loans, and secure careers. You are aware that there is pending legislation that would provide undocumented students who graduate from college legal status to live and work in the United States. You mention to the school staff that contacting their politicians and advocating for them to support this legislation would be an important strategy for reducing dropout risk factors facing their students. One of the teachers tells you, "I don't think it is appropriate for you to be talking to us about politics, they have nothing to do with the education of our children." Given what you have read about how culturally relevant, social justice–oriented prevention must attend to larger systemic forces, debate this issue in a small group. Take turns sharing how you feel about this statement. Do you agree with the teacher that this is not an appropriate issue to discuss? Why or why not? What are benefits and risks of doing so?

Learning Exercise 4: Person-Centered Versus Systemic Approach?

You have been hired by a local health maintenance organization (HMO) to develop a culturally relevant program to prevent obesity and promote healthy development among residents in an urban community. The HMO realizes that curbing obesity can have a major impact on reducing health risks and containing escalating health care claims and costs. A review of the literature reveals that school-based physical education/activity and lunch programs, the density of fast-food restaurants and convenience stores in urban neighborhoods, the presence of high levels of fats and unhealthy ingredients in packaged and fast foods, and an increased reliance on passive media activities (e.g., television, computer, etc.) as sources of entertainment have all been implicated as factors contributing to the rise in obesity. Your supervisor suggests that this understanding is too complicated and that it is best to pursue a person-centered approach that seeks to improve the health knowledge of community members and enhance their sense of personal responsibility for improving their health. Based on the literature, you understand poor health as a social justice issue and want to consider contextual systemic factors that contribute to obesity and poor health practices in the design of your prevention program. Develop a one-page rationale that outlines the basic points that you would present to your supervisor to argue that a person-centered approach would be inadequate and would ignore the contextual determinants and social justice implications of obesity. Practice this presentation with a friend or classmate.

_____ Learning Exercise 5: Who Is Community?

As discussed in this volume, involving communities as true partners in program design, implementation, and evaluation is considered an integral process for prevention programs that are culturally relevant and adhere to social justice goals. The design of a prevention program can involve multiple community partners that may not share a single perspective or program vision. With reference to the problem presented in Learning Exercise 4, you are aware that a number of personal and systemic factors contribute to the obesity epidemic. To collaborate with community partners, you must understand the perspectives of varied stakeholders. Create a table, beginning with a list of the personal and systemic factors identified in that exercise and others that you might be aware of that contribute to obesity. In the next column, for each factor, identify the stakeholder groups at the local and broader societal level that would have a vested interest in either changing or sustaining that causal factor. Review your table and discuss with a group of three to four classmates which of these "communities" need to be considered in program design, implementation, and evaluation. What do you see as the costs and benefits for ignoring any of these stakeholders? How do you determine which stakeholder groups to involve in your program design? Think of an example of how the perspective of one stakeholder group might differ from another stakeholder group.

   With the same group of students, role-play a 5-minute dialogue among stakeholders, with different stakeholder perspectives, including the prevention practitioner, assigned to different classmates. Following the 5-minute dialogue, share with one another, or the class as a whole, your reaction to the exercise, including a discussion of strategies that you might use to reconcile different perspectives.

Learning Exercise 6: A Social Justice and Culturally _____ Relevant Approach to Preventing Depression?

Within the low-income and culturally diverse community mental health agency in which you work, epidemiological data reveal that teenage mothers are at risk for depression in comparison with teenage girls who are not mothers. Your supervisor has identified an empirically supported program for the prevention of depression and is very concerned that agency resources be used to carry out a program that will be effective. She recommends that you adapt this program for use with teenage mothers in your community. You are not sure whether a depression prevention program is the best response to teenage depression in this community. Compose a one- to two-page reaction paper in which you do the following: (a) Describe how you would go about determining what type of intervention might be most helpful for teenage mothers in your community? How could a needs assessment be helpful in this process? What might this needs assessment look like? (b) Based on your needs assessment, you decide to use an empirically supported program (not necessarily a depression prevention program) as one component of your approach. You want to be sure that the program is culturally relevant for your community. Discuss how you would go about assessing the cultural relevance of the program, how you would assess whether the program is culturally relevant at a deep-structure level, and what you see as the limitations or strengths in seeking to adapt an existing program with empirical support to fit a local context.

Conclusion

Culturally relevant prevention that promotes social justice has great potential for remediating societal ills and enhancing educational and career development and physical and psychological well-being across society. In this volume, we have focused particular attention on enhancing the social and political power of those groups that have traditionally been marginalized by society in ways that contribute to health, educational, and economic disparities. Although we are committed to social justice goals, we recognize that they are inherently political and complex to achieve. In a time of economic scarcity, the need for such programs is great, but the resources to fund such efforts may be hard to find. In this volume, we describe principles of practice and evaluation, provide case examples, and offer learning exercises to prepare you for engaging in culturally relevant prevention for promoting social justice. What we have offered will provide you with a means for beginning this process. We encourage you to continue with full immersion in the other volumes of this tool kit and in maintaining current with the growing literature on this topic. We also encourage self-reflection and a willingness to look deeply at your practice. Continual engagement in dialogue with colleagues and other stakeholders, as we sought encouragement in the learning exercises of this volume, is critical for achieving culturally relevant collaboration.

References _____

Agency for Healthcare Research and Quality. (2008). *National healthcare disparities report.* Retrieved from http://www.ahrq.gov/qual/nhdr08/nhdr08.pdf

Albee, G. W. (1996). Revolutions and counterrevolutions in prevention. *American Psychologist, 51,* 1130–1133.

Albee, G. W. (2000). The Boulder model's fatal flaw. *American Psychologist, 55,* 247–248. doi:10.1037/0003-066X.55.2.247

Albee, G. W., & Ryan-Finn, K. D. (1993). An overview of primary prevention. *Journal of Counseling and Development, 72,* 115–123.

Arthur, N., & Lalande, V. (2009). Diversity and social justice implications for outcome approaches to evaluation. *International Journal of Advanced Counseling, 31,* 1–16. doi:10.1007/s10447-008-9063-z

Atkinson, D. R., Thompson, C. E., & Grant, S. K. (1993). A three-dimensional model for counseling racial/ethnic minorities. *The Counseling Psychologist, 21,* 257–277. doi:10.1177/0011000093212010

Balfanz, R. (2009). Can the American high school become an avenue of advancement for all? *Future of Children, 19,* 17–36. doi:10.1353/foc.0.0025

Bandura, A. (1997). *Self-efficacy: The exercise of control.* New York, NY: W. H Freeman/Times Books/Henry Holt.

Banyard, V. L., & Goodman, L. (2009). Collaboration for building strong communities: Two examples. In M. E. Kenny, A. M. Horne, P. Orpinas, & L. E. Reese (Eds.), *Realizing social justice: The challenge of preventive interventions* (pp. 271–287). Washington, DC: American Psychological Association.

Barrera, M., Biglan, A., Taylor, T., Gunn, B., Smolkowski, K., Black, C., . . . Fowler, R. (2002). Early elementary school intervention to reduce conduct problems: A randomized trial with Hispanic and non-Hispanic children. *Prevention Science, 3,* 83–94. doi:10.1023/A:1015443932331

Bell, L. A. (2007). Theoretical foundations for social justice education. In M. Adams, L. A. Bell, & P. Griffin (Eds.), *Teaching for diversity and social justice* (2nd ed., pp. 3–16). New York, NY: Routledge.

Bess, K. D., Prilleltensky, I., Perkins, D. D., & Collins, L. V. (2009). Participatory organizational change in community-based health and human services: From tokenism to political engagement. *American Journal of Community Psychology, 43,* 134–148. doi:10.1007/s10464-008-9222-8

Biglan, A., Mrazek, P. J., Carnine, D., & Flay, B. R. (2003). The integration of research and practice in the prevention of youth problem behaviors. *American Psychologist, 58,* 433–440. doi:10.1037/0003-066X.58.6-7.433

Bledsoe, K., & Graham, J. (2005). The use of multiple evaluation approaches in program evaluation. *American Journal of Evaluation, 26,* 302–319. doi:10.1177/1098214005278749

Blustein, D. L., Barnett, M., Mark, S., Depot, M., Lovering, M., Lee, Y., . . . DeBay, D. (2012). A longitudinal examination of high school students' exploration of STEM careers. *Journal of Career Development.* Advance online publication. doi:10.1177/08945312441680

Blustein, D. L., Juntunen, C. L., & Worthington, R. L. (2000). The school-to-work transition: Adjustment challenges of the forgotten half. In S. D. Brown & R. W. Lent (Eds.), *Handbook of counseling psychology* (3rd ed., pp. 435–470). Hoboken, NJ: Wiley.

Blustein, D., Kenna, A., Gil, N., & DeVoy, J. (2008). The psychology of working: A new framework for counseling practice and public policy. *Career Development Quarterly, 56,* 294–308.

Blustein, D. L., McWhirter, E., & Perry, J. C. (2005). An emancipatory communitarian approach to vocational development theory, research, and practice. *The Counseling Psychologist, 33,* 141–179. doi:10.1177/0011000004272268

Blustein, D., Murphy, K., Kenny, M. E., Jernigan, M., Perez-Gualdron, L., Castenda, T., . . . Davis, O. (2010). Exploring urban students' constructions about school, work, race and ethnicity. *Journal of Counseling Psychology, 57,* 248–254. doi:10.1037/a0018939

Brauner, C. B., & Stephen, B. C. (2006). Estimating the prevalence of early childhood serious emotional/behavioral disorder. *Public Health Reports, 121,* 303–310.

Bronfenbrenner, U. (1979). Contexts of child rearing: Problems and prospects. *American Psychologist, 34,* 844–850.

Buhin, L., & Vera, E. M. (2009). Preventing racism and promoting social justice: Person-centered and environment-centered interventions. *Journal of Primary Prevention, 30,* 43–59. doi:10.1007/s10935-008-0161-9

Catalano, R. F., Berglund, M. L., Ryan, J. A. M., Lonczak, H. S., & Hawkins, J. D. (2002). Positive youth development in the United States: Research findings on evaluations of positive youth development programs. *Prevention & Treatment, 5,* Article 15. Retrieved from http://psycnet.apa.org/?&fa=main.doiLanding&doi=10.1037/1522-3736.5.1.515a

Centers for Disease Control and Prevention. (2005). *Web-based injury statistics query and reporting system.* Retrieved from www.cdc.gov/ncipc/wisqars

Chaves, A., Diemer, M., Blustein, D. L., Gallagher, L., Casares, M., DeVoy, J., & Perry, J. (2004). Conceptions of work: The view from urban youth. *Journal of Counseling Psychology, 51,* 275–286.

Chávez, V., Minkler, M., Wallerstein, N., & Spencer, M. S. (2007). Community organizing for health and social justice. In L. Cohen, V. Chávez, & S. Chehimi (Eds.), *Prevention is primary: Strategies for community well-being* (pp. 95–120). San Francisco, CA: Jossey-Bass.

Chorpita, B. F. (2002). Treatment manuals in the real world: Where do we build them? *Clinical Psychology: Science and Practice, 9,* 431–433.

Cochran-Smith, M. (2000). Blind vision: Unlearning racism in teacher education. *Harvard Educational Review, 70*(2), 157–190.

Cochran-Smith, M., Gleeson, A. M., & Mitchell, K. (2010). Teacher education for social justice: What's pupil learning got to do with it? *Berkeley Review of Education, 1*(1), 35–61. Retrieved from http://escholarship.org/uc/ucbgse_bre

Cohen, L., Chávez, V., & Chehimi, S. (Eds.). (2007). *Prevention is primary: Strategies for community well-being.* San Francisco, CA: Jossey-Bass.

Cohen, L., & Wolfe, A. (2007). Working collaboratively to advance prevention. In L. Cohen, V. Chávez, & S. Chehimi (Eds.), *Prevention is primary: Strategies for community well-being* (pp. 141–160). San Francisco, CA: Jossey-Bass.

Coley, R. L., & Chase-Lansdale, P. L. (1998). Adolescent pregnancy and parenthood: Recent evidence and future directions. *American Psychologist, 53,* 152–166. doi:10.1037/0003-066X.53.2.152

Constantine, M. G., Hage, S. M., Kindaichi, M. M., & Bryant, R. M. (2007). Social justice and multicultural issues: Implications for the practice and training of counselors and counseling psychologists. *Journal of Counseling and Development, 85,* 24–29.

Conyne, R. K. (2010). *Prevention program development and evaluation: An incidence reduction, culturally relevant approach.* Thousand Oaks, CA: Sage.

Costello, E., Angold, A., Burns, B. J., Erkanli, A., Stangl, D. K., & Tweed, D. L. (1996). The Great Smoky Mountains study of youth: Functional impairment and serious emotional disturbance. *Archives of General Psychiatry, 53*(12), 1137–1143.

Crethar, H. C., Rivera, E. T., & Nash, S. (2008). In search of common threads: Linking multicultural, feminist, and social justice counseling paradigms. *Journal of Counseling and Development, 86,* 269–278.

Cutrona, C. E., & Russell, D. W. (1987). *The provisions of social relationships and adaptation to stress: Advances in personal relationships* (Vol. 1, pp. 37–67). Greenwich, CT: JAI Press.

Darling-Hammond, L. (2006). No Child Left Behind and high school reform. *Harvard Educational Review, 76,* 642–667.

De la Rosa, D., & Maw, C. (1990). *Hispanic education: A statistical portrait.* Washington, DC: National Council of La Raza.

Delgado, R., & Stefancic, J. (2001). *Critical race theory: An introduction.* New York: New York University Press.

Dryfoos, J. (1990). *Adolescents at risk: Prevalence and prevention.* New York, NY: Oxford University Press.

Elze, D. E. (2003). Gay, lesbian, and bisexual youths' perceptions of their high school environments and comfort in school. *Children and Schools, 25,* 225–239.

Evans, S. D., Hanlin, C. E., & Prilleltensky, I. (2007). Blending ameliorative and transformative approaches in human service organizations: A case study. *Journal of Community Psychology, 35,* 329–346. doi:10.1002/jcop.20172

Fetterman, D. M. (1996). Empowerment evaluation: An introduction to theory and practice. In D. M. Fetterman, S. J. Kaftarian, & A. Wandersman (Eds.), *Empowerment evaluation: Knowledge and tools for self-assessment and accountability* (pp. 3–49). Thousand Oaks, CA: Sage.

Field, J. E., & Baker, S. (2004). Defining and examining school counselor advocacy. *Professional School Counseling, 8,* 56–63.

Fine, M., & Torre, M. E. (2006). Intimate details: Participatory action research in prison. *Action Research, 4*(3), 253–269. doi:2006-11635-00210.1177/14767 50306066801

Fondacaro, M. R., & Weinberg, D. (2002). Concepts of social justice in community psychology: Towards a social psychological epistemology. *American Journal of Community Psychology, 30,* 473–492. doi:10.1023/A:1015803817117

Fouad, N. A., Gerstein, L. H., & Toporek, R. L. (2006). *Social justice and counseling psychology in context.* In R. L. Toporek, L. H. Gerstein, N. A. Fouad, G. Rosircar, & T. Israel (Eds.), *Handbook for social justice in counseling psychology: Leadership, vision, and action* (pp. 1–16). Thousand Oaks, CA: Sage.

Freire, P. (1972). *Pedagogy of the oppressed.* New York, NY: Penguin Books.

Giles, W. H., & Liburd, L. C. (2007). Achieving health equity and social justice. In L. Cohen, V. Chávez, & S. Chehimi (Eds.), *Prevention is primary: Strategies for community well-being* (pp. 25–40). San Francisco, CA: Jossey-Bass.

Goodenow, C. (1993). The psychological sense of school membership among adolescents: Scale development and educational correlates. *Psychology in the Schools, 30,* 79–90. doi:10.1002/1520-6807(199301)30:1<79::AID-PITS2310300113> 3.0.CO;2-X

Goodenow, C., & Grady, K. E. (1993).The relationship of school belonging and friends' values to academic motivation among urban adolescent students. *Journal of Experimental Education, 62*(1), 60–71.

Goodman, L., Liang, B., Helms, J., Latta, R., Sparks, E., & Weintraub, S. R. (2004). Training counseling psychologists as social justice agents: Feminist and multicultural principles in action. *The Counseling Psychologist, 32,* 793–836. doi:10.1177/0011000004268802

Gosin, M., Marsiglia, F. F., & Hecht, M. L. (2003). Keepin' it R.E.A.L: A drug resistance curriculum tailored to the strengths and needs of pre-adolescents of the southwest. *Journal of Drug Education, 33,* 119–142. doi:10.2190/DXB9-1V2P-C27J-V69V

Gottlieb, S. (1975). Psychology and the "Treatment Rights Movement." *Professional Psychology, 6,* 243–251.

Hage, S. (2000). The role of counseling psychology in preventing male violence against female intimates. *The Counseling Psychologist, 28,* 797–828.

Hage, S., Romano, J., Conyne, R., Kenny, M., Matthews, C., Schwartz, J., & Waldo, M. (2007). Best practice guidelines on prevention in practice, research, training, and social advocacy for psychologists. *The Counseling Psychologist, 35,* 493–566. doi:10.1177/0011000006291411

Harlow, C. (2003). *Education and correctional populations.* Bureau of Justice Statistics Special Report. Washington, DC: U.S. Department of Justice.

Harter, S. (1985). *Manual for the social support scale for children and adolescents.* Unpublished manuscript. University of Denver, Denver, CO.

Harvard Civil Rights Project. (2004). *Losing our future: How minority youth are being left behind by the graduation rate crisis.* Cambridge, MA: The Civil Rights Project at Harvard University.

Helms, J. E. (Ed.). (1990). *Black and white racial identity: Theory, research, and practice.* Eastport, CT: Greenwood Press.

Helms, J. E., & Cook, D. A. (1999). *Using race and culture in counseling and psychotherapy: Theory and process.* Needham Heights, MA: Allyn & Bacon.

Henggeler, S. W. (1995). Home-based delivery of multisystemic therapy: Removing barriers to treatment access for youth with serious clinical problems and their families. *Child, Youth, and Family Services Quarterly, 18,* 2–3.

Henggeler, S. W., & Lee, T. (2003). Multisystemic treatment of serious clinical problems. In A. E. Kazdin & J. R. Weisz (Eds.), *Evidence-based psychotherapies for children and adolescents* (pp. 301–322). New York, NY: Guilford Press.

Hoagwood, K. (2001). Evidence-based practice in children's mental health services: What do we know? Why aren't we putting it to use? *Report on Emotional & Behavioral Disorders in Youth, 1,* 84–88.

Huey, S. J., & Polo, A. J. (2008). Evidence-based psychosocial treatments for ethnic minority youth. *Journal of Clinical Child and Adolescent Psychology, 37,* 262–301. doi:10.1080/15374410701820174

Jacobs, F., & Goldberg, J. (2009). Evaluating contemporary social programs: Challenges and opportunities. In M. E. Kenny, A. M. Horne, P. Orpinas, & L. E. Reese (Eds.), *Realizing social justice: The challenge of preventive interventions* (pp. 97–122). Washington, DC: American Psychological Association.

Jensen, P., Hoagwood, K., & Trickett, E. (1999). Ivory towers or earthen trenches? Community collaborations to foster "real world" research. *Applied Developmental Science, 3,* 206–212. doi:10.1207 /s1532480xads0304_4

Jerald, C. (2009). *Defining a 21st century education.* Alexandria, VA: Center for Public Education. Retrieved from http://www.centerforpubliceducation.org/Learn-About/21st-Century/Defining-a-21st-Century-Education-Full-Report-PDF.pdf

Kenny, M. E., & Bledsoe, M. (2005). Contributions of the relational context to career adaptability among urban adolescents. *Journal of Vocational Behavior, 66,* 257–272. doi:10.1016/j.jvb.2004.10.002

Kenny, M. E., Blustein, D., Chaves, A., Grossman, J., & Gallagher, L. A. (2003). The role of perceived barriers and relational support in the educational and vocational lives of urban high school students. *Journal of Counseling Psychology, 20,* 142–155. doi:10.1037/0022-0167.50.2.142

Kenny, M. E., Blustein, D. L., Haase, R. F., Jackson, J., & Perry, J. (2006). Setting the stage: Career development and the school engagement process. *Journal of Counseling Psychology, 53,* 272–279. doi:10.1037/0022-0167.53.2.272

Kenny, M. E., Bower, M. E., Perry, J. C., Blustein, D. L., & Amtzis, A. (2004). *The Tools for Tomorrow program: A school-to-career intervention.* Unpublished curriculum. Boston College Lynch School of Education, Chestnut Hill, MA.

Kenny, M., & Gallagher, L. (2000). Service learning as a vehicle in training psychologists for revised professional roles. In F. T. Sherman & W. R. Torbert (Eds.), *Transforming social inquiry, transforming social action* (pp. 189–206). Norwell, MA: Kluwer Academic.

Kenny, M. E., Gualdron, L., Scanlon, D., Sparks, E., Blustein, D., & Jernigan, M. (2007). Urban adolescents' construction of supports and barriers to their educational and career attainment. *Journal of Counseling Psychology, 54,* 336–343. doi:10.1037/0022-0167.54.3.336

Kenny, M. E., & Hage, S. M. (2009). The next frontier: Prevention as an instrument of social justice. *Journal of Primary Prevention, 30,* 1–10. doi:10.1007/s10935-008-0163-7

Kenny, M. E., Horne, A. M., Orpinas, P., & Reese, L. E. (Eds.). (2009a). *Realizing social justice: The challenge of preventive interventions.* Washington, DC: American Psychological Association.

Kenny, M. E., Horne, A. M., Orpinas, P., & Reese, L. E. (2009b). Social justice and the challenge of preventive interventions: An introduction. In M. E. Kenny, A. M. Horne, P. Orpinas, & L. E. Reese (Eds.), *Realizing social justice: The challenge of preventive interventions.* (pp. 3–14). Washington, DC: American Psychological Association.

Kenny, M. E., & Romano, J. (2009). Promoting positive development and social justice through prevention: A legacy for the future. In M. E. Kenny, A. M. Horne, P. Orpinas, & L. E. Reese (Eds.), *Realizing social justice: The challenge of preventive interventions* (pp. 17–35). Washington, DC: American Psychological Association.

Kenny, M. E., Sparks, E., & Jackson, J. (2007). Striving for social justice through interprofessional university school collaboration. In E. Aldarondo (Ed.), *Advancing social justice through clinical practice* (pp. 313–335). Mahwah, NJ: Lawrence Erlbaum.

Kiselica, M., & Robinson, M. (2001). Bringing advocacy counseling to life: The history, issues, and human dramas of social justice work in counseling. *Journal of Counseling and Development, 79,* 387–397.

Koegel, L. K., Koegel, R. L., & Dunlap, G. (1996). *Positive behavioral support.* Baltimore, MD: Brookes.

Koniak-Griffin, D., Lesser, J., Nyamathi, A., Uman, G., Stein, J. A., & Cumberland, W. G. (2003). Project CHARM: An HIV prevention program for adolescent mothers. *Family & Community Health, 26,* 94–107.

Kraemer, K. L. (2007). The cost-effectiveness and cost-benefit of screening and brief intervention for unhealthy alcohol use in medical settings. *Substance Abuse, 28,* 67–77.

Kumpfer, K. L., Alvarado, R., Smith, P., & Bellamy, N. (2002). Cultural sensitivity and adaptation in family based interventions. *Prevention Science, 3,* 241–246. doi:10.1023/A:1019902902119

Lapan, R. (2004). *Career development across the K-16 years: Bridging the present to satisfying and successful futures.* Alexandria, VA: American Counseling Association.

Lee, C. C. (2002). The impact of belonging to a high school gay/straight alliance. *High School Journal, 85,* 13–26. doi:10.1353/hsj.2002.0005

Lerner, R. M. (1995). *America's youth in crisis: Challenges and options for programs and policies.* Thousand Oaks, CA: Sage.

Lerner, R. M. (2001). Promoting promotion in the development of prevention science. *Applied Developmental Science, 5,* 254–257.

Lerner, R. M., Almerigi, J., Theokas, C., & Lerner, J. V. (2005). Positive youth development: A view of the issues. *Journal of Early Adolescence, 25*(1), 10–16. doi:10.1177/0272431604273211

Lerner, R. M., & Overton, W. F. (2008). Exemplifying the integrations of the relational developmental system. *Journal of Adolescent Research, 23,* 245–255. doi:10.1177/0743558408314385

Lewis, J. A., Lewis, M. D., Daniels, J. A., & D'Andrea, M. J. (1998). *Community counseling: Empowerment strategies for a diverse society.* Pacific Grove, CA: Brooks/Cole.

MacIver, M. A., & MacIver, D. J. (2010). How do we ensure that everyone graduates? An integrated prevention and tiered intervention model for schools and districts. *New Directions for Youth Development, 127,* 25–35. doi:10.1002/yd.360

Martin-Baró, I. (1994). *Writings for a liberation psychology.* Cambridge, MA: Harvard University Press.

Masten, A. (2001). Ordinary magic: Resilience processes in development. *American Psychologist, 56,* 227–238. doi:10.1037/0003-066X.56.3.227

Matthews, C., Pepper, S., & Lorah, P. (2009). Fostering a healthy climate for diversity. In M. E. Kenny, A. M. Horne, P. Orpinas, & L. E. Reese (Eds.), *Realizing social justice: The challenge of preventive interventions* (pp. 165–184). Washington, DC: American Psychological Association.

McWhirter, E. H., Rasheed, S., & Crothers, M. (2000). The effects of high school career education on social–cognitive variables. *Journal of Counseling Psychology, 47,* 330–341. doi:10.1037/0022-0167.47.3.330

Mertens, D. L. (2003). The inclusive view of evaluation: Visions for the new millennium. In S. I. Donaldson & M. Scriven (Eds.), *Evaluating social programs and problems: Visions for the new millennium* (pp. 91–108). Mahwah, NJ: Lawrence Erlbaum.

Midgley, C., Maehr, M., Hruda, L., Anderman, E., Anderman, L., Freeman, K., . . . Urdan, T. (1997). *Manual for the patterns of adaptive learning scales.* Ann Arbor: University of Michigan.

Mitchell, K. (2011, April). *Uncovering troubling issues of institutionalized racism and linguicism in teacher preparation and beyond.* Paper presented at the annual meeting of the American Educational Research Association, New Orleans, LA.

Myers, L. J. (1988). *Understanding an Afrocentric world view: Introduction to an optimal psychology.* Dubuque, IA: Kendall.

Nakkula, M. J., & Harris, J. T. (2005). Assessment of mentoring relationships. In D. L. DuBois & M. J. Karcher (Eds.), *Handbook of youth mentoring* (pp. 100–117). Thousand Oaks, CA: Sage.

Nation, M., Crusto, C., Wandersman, A., Kumpfer, K. L., Seybolt, D., Morrissey-Kane, E., & Davino, K. (2003). What works in prevention: Principles of effective prevention programs. *American Psychologist, 58,* 449-456. doi:10.1037/0003-066X.58.6-7.449

National Science Board. (2008). *Science and engineering indicators 2008* (Vols. 1 & 2) Arlington, VA: Author.

O'Brien, K. (1992). *Career aspirations scale.* Unpublished manuscript. University of Maryland, College Park, MD.

Ostrom, C. W., Lerner, R. M., & Freel, M. A. (1995). Building the capacity of youth and families through university-community collaborations: The Development-In-Context Evaluation (DICE) model. *Journal of Adolescent Research, 10*(4), 427–448. doi:10.1177/0743554895104001

Partnership for 21st Century Skills. (2008). *21st century skills, education & competitiveness.* Tucson, AZ: Author.

Pedersen, P. (1990). The multicultural perspective as a fourth force in counseling. *Journal of Mental Health Counseling, 12,* 93–95.

Phinney, J. (1993). A three-stage model of ethnic identity development. In M. Bernal & G. Knight (Eds.), *Ethnic identity: Formation and transmission among Hispanics and other minorities* (pp. 61–79). Albany: State University of New York Press.

Pittman, K. J., Irby, M., Tolman, J., Yohalem, N., & Ferber, T. (2001). *Preventing problems, promoting development, encouraging engagement: Competing priorities or inseparable goals.* Retrieved from http://casel.org/publications/preventing-problems-promoting-development-encouraging-engagement-competing-priorities-or-inseparable-goals/

Prilleltensky, I. (1997). Values, assumptions, and practices: Assessing the moral implications of psychological discourse and action. *American Psychologist, 52*(5), 517–535. doi:10.1037/0003-066X.52.5.517

Prilleltensky, I. (2008). The role of power in wellness, oppression, and liberation: The promise of psychopolitical validity. *Journal of Community Psychology, 36,* 116–136.

Prilleltensky, I., Dokecki, P., Frieden, G., & Wang, V. O. (2007). Counseling for wellness and justice: Foundations and ethical dilemmas. In E. Aldarondo (Ed.), *Advancing social justice through clinical practice* (pp. 19–42). Mahwah, NJ: Lawrence Erlbaum.

Ramirez, M. (1999). *Psychotherapy and counseling with minorities*. Boston, MA: Allyn & Bacon.

Reese, L. E., & Vera, E. M. (2007). Culturally relevant prevention programs: Scientific and practical considerations. *The Counseling Psychologist, 35,* 763–778. doi:10.1177/0011000007304588

Reese, L. E., Vera, E. M., & Caldwell, L. (2005). The role of culture in violence prevention practice and science: Issues for consideration. In J. K. Lutzker (Ed.), *Preventing violence* (pp. 259–278). Washington, DC: American Psychological Association.

Reiss, D., & Price, R. H. (1996). National research agenda for prevention research: The National Institute of Mental Health Report. *American Psychologist, 51,* 1109–1115. doi:10.1037/0003-066X.51.11.1109

Resnicow, K., Solar, R., Braithwaite, R., Ahluwalia, J., & Butler, J. (2000). Cultural sensitivity in substance abuse prevention. *Journal of Community Psychology, 28,* 271–290. doi:10.1002/(SICI)1520-6629(200005)28:3<271::AID-JCOP4>3.0.CO;2-I

Ringel, J. S., & Sturm, R. (2001). National estimates of mental health utilization and expenditures for children in 1998. *Journal of Behavioral Health Services & Research, 28*(3), 319–333. doi:10.1007/BF02287247

Rogers, J., Morrell, E., & Enyedy, N. (2007). Contexts for becoming critical researchers: Designing for identities and creating new learning opportunities. *American Behavioral Scientist, 51,* 419–443.

Romano, J., & Netland, J. D. (2008). The application of the theory of reasoned action and planned behavior to prevention science in counseling psychology. *The Counseling Psychologist, 36,* 777–806.

Rosencrans, A., Gittlesohn, J., Ho, L., Harris, S., Naqushbandi, M., & Sharma, S. (2008). Process evaluation of a multi-institutional community-based program for diabetes prevention among First Nations. *Health Education Research, 23,* 272–286.

Rosenthal, M. S., Ross, J. S., Bilodeau, R., Richter, R. S., Palley, J. E., & Bradley, E. H. (2009). Economic evaluation of a comprehensive teenage pregnancy prevention program. *American Journal of Preventive Medicine, 37,* S280–S287.

Ruger, J. P., & Emmons, K. M. (2008). Economic evaluations of smoking cessation and relapse prevention programs for pregnant women: A systematic review. *Value in Health, 11,* 180–190.

Schweinhart, L. J., Montie, J., Xiang, Z., Barnett, W. S., Belfield, C. R., & Nores, M. (2005). *Lifetime effects: The HighScope Perry Preschool study through age 40* (Monographs of the HighScope Educational Research Foundation, 14). Ypsilanti, MI: HighScope Press.

Shore, M. (1994). Narrowing prevention. *Readings. A Journal of Reviews and Commentary in Mental Health, September,* 13–17.

Smith, L., Davis, K., & Bhowmik, M. (2010). Youth participatory action research groups as a school counseling interventions. *Professional School Counseling, 14*(2), 174–182.

Smith, T., & Silva, L. (2011). Ethnic identity and personal well-being of persons of color: A meta-analysis. *Journal of Counseling Psychology, 58,* 42–60. doi:10.1037/a0021528

Snell, P., Nola, M., & East, J. (2009). Changing directions: Participatory action research as a parent involvement strategy. *Educational Action Research, 17*(2), 239–258. doi:10.1080/09650790902914225

Solberg, V. S., Howard, K. A., Blustein, D. L., & Close, W. (2002). Career development in the schools: Connecting school-to-work-to life. *The Counseling Psychologist, 30*, 705–725. doi:10.1177/0011000002305003

Speight, S. L., Myers, L. J., Cox, C., & Highlen, P. S. (1991). A redefinition of multicultural counseling. *Journal of Counseling & Development, 70*, 29–36.

Speight, S., & Vera, E. (2004). Social justice: Ready or not? *The Counseling Psychologist, 32*, 109–118. doi:10.1177/0011000003260005

Speight, S. L., & Vera, E. M. (2008). Social justice and counseling psychology. In R. Lent & S. Brown (Eds.), *Handbook of counseling psychology* (pp. 54–67). Hoboken, NJ: Wiley.

Stevens, E., & Wood, G. H. (1992). *Justice, ideology, and education: An introduction to the social foundations of education.* New York, NY: McGraw-Hill.

Stringer, E. (2004). *Action research in education.* Upper Saddle River, NJ: Pearson.

Sue, D. W., & Sue, D. (1999). *Counseling the culturally different: Theory and practice.* Hoboken, NJ: Wiley.

Sum, A. (2008). *Getting to the finish line: College enrollment and graduation. A seven year longitudinal study of the Boston Public Schools class of 2008.* Boston, MA: Northeastern University Center for Labor Market Studies. Retrieved from http://www.bostonpublicschools.org/files/Getting%20to%20 the%20Finish%20Line.pdf

Super, D. E., Thompson, A. S., Lindeman, R. H., Jordaan, J. P., & Myers, R. A. (1981). *The career development inventory.* Palo Alto, CA: Consulting Psychologists Press.

Taylor, R. D., Casten, R., & Flickinger, S. M. (1993). Influence of kinship social support on the parenting experiences and psychosocial adjustment of African-American adolescents. *Developmental Psychology, 29*, 382–388. doi:10.1037/ 0012-1649.29.2.382

Toporek, R. L., Gerstein, L. H., Fouad, N. A., Roysircar, G., & Israel, T. (2006). Future directions for counseling psychology: Enhancing leadership, vision, and action in social justice. In R. L. Toporek, L. H. Gerstein, N. A. Fouad, G. Rosircar, & T. Israel (Eds.), *Handbook for social justice in counseling psychology: Leadership, vision, and action* (pp. 533–552). Thousand Oaks, CA: Sage.

Toporek, R. L., Lewis, J. A., & Crethar, H. C. (2009). Promoting systemic change through the ACA advocacy competencies. *Journal of Counseling and Development, 87*, 260–268.

Trickett, E. (2007). George Albee and the nurturing spirit of primary prevention. *Journal of Primary Prevention, 28*, 61–64.

Trusty, J., & Brown, D. (2005). Advocacy competencies for professional school counselors. *Professional School Counseling, 8*, 259–265.

Upshur, C., & Barreto-Cortez, E. (1995). What is participatory evaluation? What are its roots? *Evaluation Exchange, 1*, 7–9.

U.S. Census Bureau. (2010). *American community survey 2010.* Washington, DC: U.S. Department of Commerce.

U.S. Department of Health and Human Services. (2000). *Healthy people 2010.* Washington, DC: Government Printing Office.

Vaux, A. (1988). Social and emotional loneliness: The role of social and personal characteristics. *Personality and Social Psychology Bulletin, 14,* 722–734. doi:10.1177/0146167288144007

Vera, E. M. (2000). A recommitment to prevention in counseling psychology: Embracing our roots. *The Counseling Psychologist, 28,* 829–837. doi:10.1177/0011000000286004

Vera, E. M. (2007). Culture, prevention, and politics of disparities. *The Counseling Psychologist, 35,* 860–867. doi:10.1177/0011000007306532

Vera, E. M., Buhin, L., & Isacco, A. (2009). The role of prevention in psychology's social justice agenda. In M. E. Kenny, A. M. Horne, P. Orpinas, & L. E. Reese (Eds.), *Realizing social justice: The challenge of preventive interventions* (pp. 79–96). Washington, DC: American Psychological Association.

Vera, E. M., Daly, B., Gonzalez, R., Morgan, M., & Thakral, C. (2006). Prevention and outreach with underserved populations. In R. L. Toporek, L. Gerstein, N. Fouad, G. Roysircar, & T. Isreal (Eds.), *Handbook for social justice in counseling psychology: Leadership, vision, and action* (pp. 86–99). Thousand Oaks, CA: Sage.

Vera, E. M., & Speight, S. L. (2003). Multicultural competence, social justice, and counseling psychology: Expanding our roles. *The Counseling Psychologist, 31,* 253–272. doi:10.1177/0011000003031003001

Voelkl, K. E. (1997). Identification with school. *American Journal of Education, 105,* 294–318.

Vondracek, F. W., Lerner, R. M., & Schulenberg, J. W. (1986). *Career development: A life-span developmental approach.* Hillsdale, NJ: Lawrence Erlbaum.

Walsh, M. E., DePaul, J., & Park-Taylor, J. (2009). Prevention as a mechanism for promoting positive development in a context of risk: Addressing the risk and protective factors of our cultures. In M. E. Kenny, L. E. Reese, A. M. Home, & P. Orpinas (Eds.), *Realizing social justice: The challenge of preventive intervention* (pp. 57–78). Washington, DC: American Psychological Association.

Watts, R., Abdul-Adil, J., & Pratt, T. (2002). Enhancing critical consciousness in young African American men: A psychoeducational approach. *Psychology of Men and Masculinity, 3,* 41–50.

Webster-Stratton, C. (1992a). *The incredible years: A troubleshooting guide for parents of children aged 3–8.* Toronto, Ontario, Canada: Umbrella Press.

Webster-Stratton, C. (1992b). *The teachers and children's videotape series: Dina dinosaur's social skills and problem-solving curriculum.* Seattle, WA: Incredible Years.

Weisfeld, A., & Perlman, R. L. (2005). Disparities and discrimination in health care: An introduction. *Perspectives in Biology and Medicine, 48*(1), S1–S9. doi:10.1353/pbm.2005.0046

Wight, D., & Obasi, A. (2002). Unpacking the "black box:" The importance of process data to explain outcomes. In J. Stephenson, J. Imrie, & C. Bonell (Eds.), *Effective sexual health interventions: Issues in experimental evaluation* (pp. 151–166). Oxford, England: Oxford University Press.

Wilson, S. J., Lipsey, M. W., & Derzon, J. H. (2003). The effects of school-based intervention programs on aggressive behavior: A meta-analysis. *Journal of Consulting and Clinical Psychology, 71*(1), 136–149. doi:10.1037/0022-006X.71.1.136

Young, I. M. (1990). *Justice and the politics of difference.* Princeton, NJ: Princeton University Press.

Index

About the Authors _____

Elizabeth M. Vera is a professor in the School of Education at Loyola University Chicago, Chicago, Illinois, where she teaches courses in the counseling psychology PhD and counseling master's programs. Dr. Vera's scholarship focuses on social justice, multiculturalism, prevention, and promoting mental health and academic successes in urban adolescents of color. Dr. Vera is a Fellow of the American Psychological Association (APA) and has served as Chair of the Board of Convention Affairs and a member of the Committee on Ethnic Minority Affairs for the APA. Dr. Vera has also been active in Division 17 of APA, having served as a vice president for Diversity and Public Policy. She is the author of numerous journal articles, book chapters, and several books. She received her PhD in 1993 from The Ohio State University.

Maureen E. Kenny is professor, Department of Counseling, Developmental and Educational Psychology in the Lynch School of Education at Boston College, Massachusetts, where she has also served as Interim Dean and Associate Dean for Faculty and Academics. Dr. Kenny's scholarship focuses on the development, implementation, and evaluation of interventions that promote positive academic, career, and psychosocial development among adolescents. Dr. Kenny is an editorial board member for the *Journal of Counseling Psychology* and served as Chair of the American Psychological Association (APA) Division 17 Section on Prevention. Dr. Kenny is the author of numerous journal articles, book chapters, and books focusing on prevention, social justice, and the importance of relationships with caring adults across the adolescent years. With Drs. Andy Horne, Pamela Orpinas, and LeRoy Reese, she coedited the volume, *Realizing Social Justice: The Challenge of Preventive Interventions*, published by APA. Dr. Kenny completed an MEd in psychological counseling from Columbia University and a PhD with specializations in counseling and school psychology from the University of Pennsylvania.

$SAGE research**methods**

The essential online tool for researchers from the world's leading methods publisher

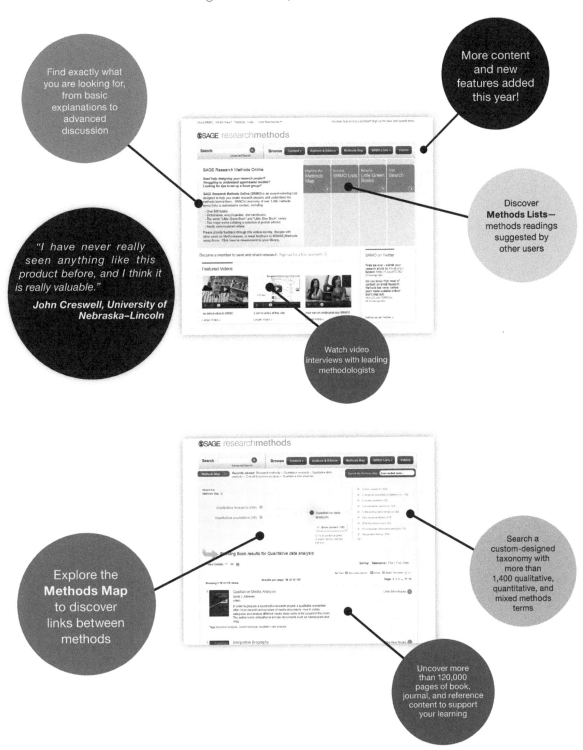

Find exactly what you are looking for, from basic explanations to advanced discussion

More content and new features added this year!

Discover **Methods Lists**— methods readings suggested by other users

"I have never really seen anything like this product before, and I think it is really valuable."

John Creswell, University of Nebraska–Lincoln

Watch video interviews with leading methodologists

Explore the **Methods Map** to discover links between methods

Search a custom-designed taxonomy with more than 1,400 qualitative, quantitative, and mixed methods terms

Uncover more than 120,000 pages of book, journal, and reference content to support your learning

Find out more at
www.sageresearchmethods.com